FROM PIECES TO PEACE

By Helen Crossland
with Judy Doyle, Ph.D.

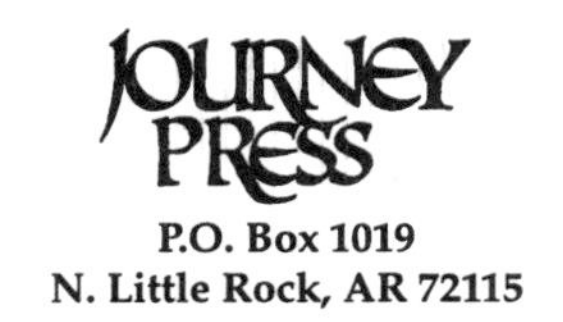

P.O. Box 1019
N. Little Rock, AR 72115

Dedication

This book is dedicated both to those whose hearts have joined with the heart of God for the ministry of Homes of Hope and the residents, the past, present, and future.

Produced by "Journey Press"
P.O. Box 1019
N. Little Rock, AR 72115

Foreward

Have you ever watched helplessly as someone you love becomes progressively entangled in behavior patterns that you believe will destroy their life and perhaps your life as well? Have you felt the slow erosion of your trust in God's love and wisdom, resulting in despair and making personal choices that strip you of all hope and self-respect? That is what happened to Helen Crossland. Because we were a part of a church staff with Don and Helen Crossland, we were witnesses as Helen's life was shattered by a sequence of tragic events. We also watched in wonder as God mercifully rebuilt her life from the foundation up, transforming the broken pieces into peace.

In this book we are granted the privilege of watching Helen being taught of the Lord step by step, acquiring the practical principles for experiencing the peace in which she walks today. We saw Helen struggle with devastating rejection and betrayal, shame and misunderstanding, yet making the decision to choose growth. We saw her commit herself to risk both sorrow and joy. We watched her learn new skills, each time confronting the pain at deeper levels. As Helen openly shares herself with her readers, we see exemplified in her personal life the empowering truths she began experiencing as she walked through tragedy toward triumph.

A "how-to" book that reads like a novel, *From Pieces to Peace* will guide you in taking practical, powerful steps toward your personal destination of wholeness.

Enjoy the journey!

Gary and Norma Smalley

Preface

Every decade or so a book is written that grips the heart so poignantly that it has life changing effects. I believe that this book will do just that. Each time that I personally read the manuscript for editing or other purposes, I cried easily and rejoiced over God's grace and mercy in our marriage and life together. It brought me often to recall our pain, but more so the victories. Only recently sitting next to someone while traveling, the person said, "out of every mess comes our message, and out of every testing comes our testimony." I believe this book will show the reality to you the reader, a message and testimony of God's love.

Helen is a remarkable woman. Her growth from a seventeen year old teenage bride to the woman she now is who writes, counsels, and oversees a vital ministry, *Homes of Hope* with multiple residential houses for men and women in restoration, is a story within itself. How I can still remember almost 40 years ago, Helen trying to stand behind my six foot two inch frame trying to hide or stay unseen in public places and functions. Her own self identity was in me, her twenty year old husband and pastor. I was often surprised how timid she was in public, yet to be thrust so quickly into public responsibility as a pastor's wife and mother.

Someone recently remarked that this book should be in the hands of every woman in the world. I would add to that, I wish it could also be in the hands of every man. It is a story of our own journey together through the quagmire of sexually compulsive behavior on my part, the accompanying guilt and shame with all the characteristics of addictive behavior. I asked Helen to be honest and forthright in her writing. It is not our purpose to cover up or hide, but to be transparent, resulting in many coming to freedom and restoration.

My prayer for you, the reader, is that the Holy Spirit will use Helen's story to bring you to a place of peace and joy through Jesus Christ.

Don Crossland:

Don is the husband of Helen Crossland and has authored two books, *Journey Toward Wholeness* and *Refocusing Your Passions.* He is also the president of Journey Toward Wholeness Ministries and conducts conferences and seminars throughout the nation.

Acknowledgments

I am indebted to many for their encouragement in this book becoming a reality. Michele Buckingham verbalized it into existence. Leah Springer insisted on and arranged for Judy Doyle and I to meet. Judy Doyle is an incredible person with abilities to match. I am privileged she chose to walk with me on this venture. My husband, Don, encouraged me to press on, even though it involved us looking back on a painful past journey, when we prefer looking at, and being much more excited about, our present and future journey.

A special tribute to our children, Tamra and Rod, whose lives were forever altered by circumstances beyond their control.

With love and gratitude to the Prince of Peace who took my pieces and gave me peace.

Special thanks to:

Gary and Norma, for being forever friends.

Frances and Hank, my sister and brother in law who have walked with me through every circumstance and are a vital part of Homes of Hope Ministries.

Sueena and Larry, for their servants hearts and willingness to walk with me through thick and thin.

Frances and Jarius, who try to keep me in balance.

Dr. Wanda Stephens, who has been like a mentor, giving me opportunities to learn in ways I would never have thought possible.

Dr. David Haas, who has encouraged me to go beyond my comfort zone and develop professional skills he alone recognized in me.

Darla Haas, for initially reading and editing the manuscript and offering valuable suggestions.

For various important reasons, these people deserve to be mentioned and thanked: Sandi, Joyce, Kenny and Sharon, Barry and Sherry, Joe and Karen, Homer and Ruby, Jean, Violeta, Stan and Judy, Joe, Jamie and Jackie, Bob and Ann, Jack and Barbara, Mark and Michael, Dick and Amy, and my physical and spiritual families who have helped "hold up my arms." You are all dear to my heart.

Contents

Chapter 1

AN ULTIMATUM

"I'm warning You, God!" I raged, too angry to cry. "I'm tired of lying in bed at night with knots in my stomach, praying for You to do something to change my husband. I've fasted and prayed and waited and waited, and You still haven't done anything. I've had it! If Don gets involved with one more person, I will, too!"

There.... I'd said it, I'd meant it, and I wasn't sorry. Month after month, year after year of agonizing heartbreak, tormenting fears and shattering disappointments had left me rebellious, bitter and angry at God. How many times had I prayed, "Lord, please change my husband so I can have some peace and not be miserable. Please do something. Please..."?

Lately my pleas had grown even more desperate. "God, if Don is not going to change, please take him out of my life. I don't want to hurt people or bring shame on Your name by leaving him or asking for a divorce. Couldn't You just let him have a heart attack and die or let him get killed in a car wreck? Then I'd be free, and nobody would ever have to know about what is happening in our lives. Please God! Please do something!"

I simply didn't think I could go any further. I'd tried to be a godly woman and a good wife. I'd read every book on marriage and attended every seminar that came along. I'd become such an expert on the subject, I'd even taught in seminars! Yet in spite of all my efforts, nothing had changed. Why? Why hadn't God answered my prayers?

Furthermore, how could God continue to anoint Don's preaching and teaching when He knew all about the sin in his life? How could people continue to be blessed by my husband's ministry? How could their lives be changed ? Even though I faithfully prepared and earnestly prayed before teaching my Sunday school class, I never sensed anything close to the anointing I saw on Don's ministry. How could such a thing be?

Most Christian women in my situation could have gone to their pastors for prayer and counseling. I could have, too, except for one big problem: My husband was my pastor. I surely couldn't talk to him and, for some unfathomable reason, talking to God about my dilemma seemed to be utterly useless. That left me few options since I didn't feel comfortable about confiding in other pastors or close friends.

The few times in the past when I'd consulted counselors concerning my suspicions and anxieties, they had either politely implied or boldly stated that it was I, not my husband, who needed to change. In a way, I could understand their position. My tall, nice-looking husband's countenance mirrored the sensitive, compassionate nature inside, and his infectious smile communicated warmth and caring. He was a hard worker, a deep thinker, a great listener and a tremendously effective communicator. No wonder I'd been instantly attracted to him when our paths crossed many years before.

But the Don Crossland I'd met as a 15-year-old farm girl had been a totally different person back then. I had never dreamed he could become a cold, withdrawn stranger who now slept with his back to me, had trouble looking me in the eye and reacted in anger whenever I pressured him for explanations. The lonely man I saw in the privacy of our home without his "perfect pastor" mask bore little resemblance to the young man I'd fallen in love with so long ago....

First Impressions

New faces had always been few and far between at our small church out in West Texas. So when I saw a slender, dark-haired guy sitting in the crowd that Sunday morning during our annual youth revival, he had my full attention. I thought he was cute, and I especially liked the dimple that danced in one cheek whenever he smiled at the preacher's corny jokes.

After church, my girlfriends and I hid behind a big evergreen tree so we could get a closer peek at the bashful stranger. It hadn't taken us long to find out that his name was Don Crossland and that he'd graduated from high school a few months before coming to live with his great-aunt, whose house sat right next door to the church. He was working at his aunt's cafe, sacking groceries at a local store and working occasionally for some of the local farmers.

That Sunday evening after the preacher had led us in a community visitation program, all the teenagers of the church crowded into my parents' home for prayer and refreshments. My pulse quickened when Don walked through our living room door and sat on the piano bench right beside the child-sized chair I was occupying next to our old upright piano. But his shy glances in my older sister's direction soon betrayed the fact that he hadn't even noticed that I existed. I needn't have fretted, however. Don Crossland and I were soon to be introduced.

After arriving a few minutes late, the preacher—a plump, jolly fellow with a big, booming voice that matched his size—began entertaining the crowd by acting out how a dog had grabbed him by the pants during visitation. Unaware that Don was sitting just behind him, the preacher bent over and spun around to demonstrate exactly how and where the dog had bitten him. His ample posterior collided with the unsuspecting stranger, scooting him right off the piano bench and into my lap!

Everyone, including Don and me, roared with laughter. The incident was so ridiculous, so embarrassing, the two of us were struck with a case of uncontrollable giggles. The harder we tried to stop laughing, the more hilarious things became. It got so bad that we didn't dare look at each other during prayer time, because even the serious prayer requests got us tickled.

That next Sunday after church, Don asked if I'd like to ride with him into Lubbock, a city about 20 miles away, and get a Coke. When my parents gave their permission, I scrambled into his old Ford and off we went. During that trip and on our dates in the months ahead, Don and I began to get acquainted.

On His Own

Don wasn't easy to get close to. He said little about his past, and if he did happen to mention it, his manner was always quiet and uncondemning. However, little by little, I managed to fit the pieces together.

I learned that he was the fifth of seven children in his family. Even though his parents weren't Christians or church-goers, at the age of 12, Don had given his heart to the Lord when neighbors invited him to church. He'd begun preaching in small churches here and there when he turned 13. While such a commitment would have made many fathers proud, it displeased Don's father who, like his father before him, distrusted and disliked preachers. His father's view of "real" men seemed to be those who swore, drank and did not hide their sexual conquests. He often kept Don from church by making him work. Don's mother had become a Christian during Don's early teenage years. When her son told her of his desire to enter the Christian ministry, she was pleased. His dad, on the other hand, just stared at him in disgust and said, "You're not much of a damned man and never will be."

I also learned why Don was living with his great-aunt. A couple of months or so after Don's high school graduation, his father had come home one night in a drunken rage, cursing and warning Don he either had to give up all the stuff about religion and Jesus or leave home the next morning. Knowing his father often ranted and raved, venting his anger when he was drunk, Don hoped his dad would change his mind when he sobered up—but he didn't. Though Don had just bought a tire for his old car and had only $17 in his pocket, he felt he had no choice but to gather up his clothes and leave home. His great- aunt, who had tended to him a lot when he was a child, graciously took him in.

Will You Marry Me Someday?

The more I got to know Don Crossland, the more I liked him. He liked me, too. As a matter of fact, I was only 15 when Don first asked me to marry him. I remember he said, "Not now, but someday will you marry me?" I told him yes. From that time on, we both knew we would be married.

Don and I became engaged during my junior year, with the understanding that I would finish high school before we married. By this time he was carrying dual responsibilities as a college student and as the pastor of a small church in a nearby farming community.

Me? A Pastor's Wife?

The last semester of my junior year I took correspondence courses from Texas Tech University and earned all the extra credits I needed to complete my senior year ahead of schedule. In May of 1960, I graduated from high school and turned 17. Don and I married a month later, and I became a pastor's wife.

I knew the responsibilities I had assumed would have been heavy for a mature woman, much less a 5-foot-3-inch, 98-pound, pony-tailed teenager. Although I laughed at the good-natured jokes of those who teased me about being so young, inside I quivered with fear and feelings of inadequacy for my new role. Little did I know just how deep those inadequacies really were.

The Gift of Life

We had been married about a year and a half when our daughter Tamra was born. She brought much joy and fulfillment into our relationship, which was already very happy. Though Don and I sympathized with the problems that some of the couples we knew were having, we were so contented together we couldn't imagine what other married people found to argue and fight about. I needed my husband, and he needed me. That's not always healthy, but it works for a season if you have a vacuum in your soul—and both of us did.

One Sunday afternoon a few months after Tamra's birth, our secure world together was jolted. We were sitting at the kitchen table just finishing our lunch. Don suddenly felt a need to go check on Tamra, who was sleeping in her crib in our bedroom. All of a sudden, he screamed for me to come quickly. Before I could get to him, he came running toward our front door with Tamra in his arms. Her baby-pink face had turned dark, and she appeared lifeless.

Just as we raced out the front door toward our car, a couple from our church came driving up. They told us later that they had been eating lunch when they were prompted by a sudden, strong urge to drive over and see us. We literally dove into their back seat, and we raced toward the hospital. The woman grabbed Tamra out of Don's arms and began trying to get her to breathe. After what seemed like an eternity, we heard a small whimper. By the time we got to the hospital, Tamra was breathing normally, and color had returned to her face.

But later that evening, as I sat beside her hospital bed holding her tiny hand, Tamra stopped breathing once again. The nurse in the room grabbed her, sent for the doctor and began breathing into her mouth. Panic-stricken, Don and I literally begged God not to let her die.

From that day on I was very aware that life is fragile and uncertain. Tamra lived, but for weeks afterward I could hardly sleep. Fearful that she might stop breathing and we wouldn't be there, I hovered over her crib or jumped out of bed at the slightest sound.

Time to Move On

About a year after Tamra's birth, we accepted another pastorate. After we'd moved to Welch, a tiny town down by Lamesa, Texas, Don confided that he believed the Lord had told him we would be there exactly two years. Distracted by a busy toddler and all the work involved in unpacking and trying to turn a house into a home, I didn't think much about it at the time.

Not long after that, Don and I were elated to discover I was pregnant again. When I miscarried at 3 months, sympathetic friends patted me on the shoulder and said, "Oh, that's too bad. But you'll have another one." However, for me the experience proved to be very traumatic. It was so much more than just a "miscarriage." My tiny baby had died. I experienced deep grief, but didn't know how to talk about it to anyone. To make matters worse, doctors told me that they didn't think I could carry another baby even if by some slim chance I happened to become pregnant again.

As the two-year time period Don had mentioned earlier began drawing to a close, I asked him about what he'd told me. He shrugged and replied, "I don't know. I just think that's what God said."

Not long after that we got a call from a pastor in Lamesa who had been contacted by a church committee in Renton, Washington. "Don," he said, "I can't get you off my mind. A lot of preachers who know about this opportunity are wanting to go and would move tomorrow, but I think you're the pastor for that church."

When Don flew to Washington to check it out, he felt in his spirit that Renton was exactly where God was calling us to go. He came home, talked it over with me and we began making arrangements to move. We were both awed by the wisdom and supernatural timing of God when, exactly 2 years to the day after we'd moved into our home in Welch, the moving van arrived to move us out.

Though I was now 21, I felt like a three-year-old child being ripped out of her mother's arms as we pulled out of my parents' driveway to begin the long journey to a new home, a new state and a new church family. I sobbed until I thought my heart would literally burst. Three-year-old Tamra kept patting me on the head and pleading, "Mommy, please don't cry anymore." When that didn't work, she said, "Let's take turns. It's my turn to be the mommy and cry." Tamra didn't know it, but much of my pain came from knowing she didn't understand that we were moving so far away and that she wouldn't get to see her Me-Ma and Papa the next week, or the next, or the next. The tears flowed off and on during the entire trip.

However, we loved our new church and the breath-taking beauty surrounding us. Looking out our kitchen window and seeing the Cascade mountain range and magnificent, snow-capped Mt. Ranier made me ever aware of God's splendor. But moving 2,000 miles away from family, friends and everything with which we were familiar was quite a shock. To make matters worse, Don and I had little, if any, fellowship with other pastors and church leaders. Churches seemed competitive instead of cooperative. To help cope with the gnawing sense of isolation, Don became more involved than ever in all the multi-faceted responsibilities of building a thriving church, and I submerged myself in making a home and rearing Tamra.

I've Found Your Baby!

Our longing for another child had not diminished, so three-and-a-half years after the miscarriage, Don and I decided to begin adoption proceedings through an agency in Seattle. We were ecstatic when the case worker called and exclaimed, "I have found your baby!" She was right. The moment Don and I saw the precious 5-month-old boy with big blue eyes and light brown hair, he stole our hearts. We knew he was ours.

We named our baby Brad. Tamra absolutely adored her new little brother. He was a thousand times more lovable and fun to play with than any doll she had, and Brad seemed to thrive on her mothering as the months passed. It seemed as if he had always been part of our family. No matter how tired Don was when he walked through our front door, his eyes lit up as Brad came running and threw himself into his daddy's arms. In fathering Brad, Don was discovering the joy of a special father-son bond he had never known with his own dad.

Little Brad loved to munch on strips of bacon left over from breakfast as he roamed about the house. Everywhere he went, his chubby hands left behind a trail of greasy fingerprints. Very much aware that God had saved Brad for our family, I treasured every precious little smudge, waiting until the sliding glass door leading out to the back porch was smeared with handprints before reaching for my Windex and paper towels. I couldn't imagine life without him.

He's A Sick Little Cookie

On a crisp September morning when Brad was 15 months old, Don and I were lying in bed and Brad was jumping up and down between us. Suddenly his body went limp and he began convulsing. He'd had problems with allergies and asthma since he was born, and sometimes experienced difficulty in breathing, but a convulsion was something totally different. Once the frightening spasms subsided, we didn't think Brad was responding as he should, so we took him to the doctor.

After examining him, the doctor said, "He's a sick little cookie, all right, but he's not going to die or anything like that. However, I want to put him in the hospital just to observe him and do a blood test, if that's okay with you."

Don and I readily agreed. To our relief, the results of the blood test taken that Saturday morning were normal. But the results of the blood test taken Sunday morning were another story. That test revealed the presence of meningococcus, a bacterium that causes cerebrospinal meningitis, an infectious disease that's usually fatal within 24 hours. Brad hadn't had the problem when he'd entered the hospital. How had he contracted it?

Peace With God

The medical team began a fierce, heroic fight to save Brad's life. As they cut into a vein in his chubby little leg so one million units of penicillin could be put directly into his blood stream, I felt a calm, a sense of security. Just the week before I had prayed, and for the first time in my life, I had consciously, deliberately given my family to God. After all, who knew better how to take care of my loved ones than God Himself? The doctor's reassuring words also echoed in my ears: "He's a sick little cookie, all right, but he's not going to die, or anything like that." I knew our baby would be okay.

As I stood beside Brad's bed, longing to hold him but knowing I couldn't because of the tubes winding into his body, I suddenly felt prompted to pick up the Bible on the bedside table. I let it fall open. My eyes were instantly drawn to a passage in Romans 5:

> Therefore having been justified by faith, we have peace with God through our Lord Jesus Christ,
>
> through whom also we have obtained our introduction by faith into this grace in which we stand; and we exult in hope of the glory of God.
>
> And not only this, but we also exult in our tribulations, knowing that tribulation brings about perseverance;
>
> and perseverance, proven character; and proven character, hope;
>
> and hope does not disappoint, because the love of God has been poured out within our hearts through the Holy Spirit who was given to us...(Rom. 5: 1-5, NAS).

All day long I kept reading those verses over and over until I knew them by heart. Phrase by phrase, the words went from my head into my spirit.

Late that night when the nurses called the doctor into the room, I was still engulfed by a sense of calm and security. I saw that the doctor was really in a panic, but I was so naive about death, I didn't know how to read the danger signals. The nurse's worried comments about Brad's blood pressure dropping meant nothing to me.

Just before midnight, Brad stopped breathing. I stared at the doctor and waited. I didn't say a word, but inside I was pleading, urging, "Do something. He's got to breathe. He can't live if he doesn't breathe. Do something!"

I'm sure it was the frantic look on our faces that caused the doctor to massage Brad's chest for several minutes. Finally, the doctor's tear-filled eyes met ours and he said in a choked whisper, "I'm sorry.... There's nothing else I can do." The awful truth hit me. The doctor wasn't a miracle worker. Brad had died, and he couldn't make him come back....

Overcome with grief, I ran to a phone to call my parents. The 2,000 miles between us seemed like 2 million at that moment. I remember sobbing uncontrollably and saying over and over, "He just couldn't make it. He just couldn't make it. He tried so hard, but he just couldn't make it."

I had watched life go out of our baby, and I had been powerless to do anything about it. Yet deep inside my broken heart and I could hear the words, "...But you have peace with God.... Peace with God.... Peace with God...."

In the days that followed, those words continued to calm my devastated spirit. Without them, I'm quite sure I would have become bitter. The doctor told us that the meningococcus bacterium is especially prevalent in hospital nurseries and that, in all probability, one of the nurses tending Brad had neglected to wash her hands, bringing the deadly bacteria into our son's room.

Peace with God.... Peace with God.... Somehow, those words helped me forgive the careless nurse and kept me from becoming angry at the doctor for triggering a false sense of security in my heart. How could he know what faith I'd placed in his confident, reassuring words: "Oh, he's a sick little cookie, all right, but he's not going to die or anything like that"?

How Do You Say "Goodbye"?

The next days were a blur as we went through all the unwelcome, but necessary, motions. Calling our families. Going to the funeral home to select a little casket. Choosing which special little suit we would bury our tiny angel in. Deciding whom to ask to speak at his funeral. And on and on and on....

After the funeral our families left, one by one. All that Don,

Tamra and I had left of our precious little Brad were his pictures, clothes and toys, our memories and a mountain of staggering grief to surmount. And I had one more agonizing, yet precious, reminder of my little mess-maker: a trail of greasy, little fingerprints winding from the sliding glass door to the hall walls.

By this time, Don and I had been married almost 8 years. He had preached dozens of funerals, and as a couple we had tried to extend comfort to more tearful faces than we could bear to recall. But now, Death had hung an awful black wreath on the door of our own hearts, and we had no idea how to ever become whole again.

We had never had anyone model a healthy grieving process for us. On top of that obstacle, just two weeks after Brad's death, Don and I slipped into a prayer service in another church and listened in stunned silence as a well-known minister declared, "God never let a child die if the parents had enough faith." I felt as if he had thrown a dagger and pierced my heart. I sobbed all the way home. Later, it dawned upon me that the average believer receives little or no practical teaching from the church on how to die or how to deal with death.

Tamra fought her own battle with God as reality set in days after Brad's burial. Kneeling beside Brad's empty crib, Tamra told God she was tired of pretending that Brad had gone away on a long trip, even though her mom and dad had told her that her brother was in heaven. "I'm ready to get Brad back," she whispered tearfully. "I'm gonna close my eyes and count to 10. When I say 10, I want You to put Brad back in his bed." She began to count, ever so slowly, her faith increasing with every number. Finally, it was time to open her eyes. "Ten!" Expecting to see Brad's smiling face peering at her over his crib, Tamra looked up. But God hadn't answered. After trying again and again, she burst into tears and ran out of the room.[1]

As for me, I wasn't winning my unending war with grief, either. All the pain I had felt after miscarrying at home all alone years before came flooding back. I remembered standing dumbstruck, helplessly holding the fragile form of a 3-month-old fetus in my palm and wondering what to do with the tiny body of a baby with no name whom I had already grown to love. I simply could not bring myself to flush it down the toilet

---

[1]Tamra Vines, "Textures of the Heart: My Journey Through Grief," (P.O. Box 1231, Euless, Texas 76039, c 1994).

or throw it away. Finally, I gently wrapped the baby in a Kleenex, placed it in a baby food jar and put the jar in my purse. Though no one knew, for a while, life passed by in a blur of tears. I felt that no one related to my loss. Weeks later when I went to the doctor, I gave the baby to him, knowing in my heart that he would do for me what I had been unable to do.

But there was no one to whom I could surrender my burden of grief for Brad. My baby boy was gone, and yet he was everywhere I looked. Somehow, ever so slowly, I managed to box up his clothes and toys and take down his crib. But the precious little fingerprints and handprints.... How could I give them up? They were all I had left of Brad now, and they were everywhere. On the windows and the sliding glass door. On the furniture. Here and there along the walls....

I'd sit in the floor, sobbing and staring at a particular tiny handprint. Then slowly, deliberately, I'd force myself to wipe it away. Over a period of months as I was able to part with one precious smudge, then another, my broken heart slowly began to mend.

Drifting Apart

I was working through my grief, but my husband was not healing. To those who did not know him as I did, he seemed okay on the outside. But inside he was a hemorrhaging mass of hurt. I felt his pain and longed to help him, but I didn't know how.

It didn't take me long to realize that the death of a child can do strange things to families. Communication between Don and me became strained. He threw every ounce of available energy into the church. It was as if bigger numbers and better programs were becoming idols to him. When Don was home, he dropped out of reality by absorbing himself in a book. Before long, he was plowing through five or more books a week. They were all good books—church history, material he could use for sermons, etc., but I could sense that he was pulling away. Feeling misunderstood and rejected, I withdrew too, and we drifted further apart.

Stress, Suspicions and Excuses

To complicate matters even more, our house was constantly filled with activity. Several Sunday school classes met in our home, and people seemed to be constantly coming and going. I'd always had a tendency to be the caregiver who took care of others' problems, and problems were one thing people never had a shortage of. I waged a never-ending war, trying to find the right balance between ministering to others and taking care of my responsibilities as a wife and mother. One stress piled upon another until I thought I couldn't handle another one.

Then Don began to be away from home more and more. Several hours of unexplained absence during the day.... Coming in later in the evenings.... Whenever I pressed him for an explanation, he'd just shrug and say he'd driven into Seattle to visit the library or that he'd been driving around, praying and trying to sort out his thoughts. Since Don had always been a "book-aholic" and could absolutely lose himself in a dusty old bookstore or a library, I didn't think too much about it at first. But I began to be troubled by a vague uneasiness, a steadily growing certainty that all was not right with my husband.

My own insecurities really began surfacing at this point. My identity was in my husband. He had become my life source. The more he pulled away, the more I panicked, grasping at ways to keep him close to me.

I was uncomfortable with the behavior patterns I saw emerging in my husband. However, if I tried to talk about them, he managed to come up with a legitimate-sounding excuse or say something that resulted in me feeling guilty for harboring doubts and suspicions. Gradually, as the unfamiliar became the ordinary, I fell into the trap of assuming that what was familiar was normal. After all, if you've never been around a genuinely healthy, whole relationship, how do you know if you have one?

When I thought about my husband's patterns of behavior, it was easy to rationalize them away. Ever since I'd known Don, he'd had a restless, wandering way about him. Unless he was absorbed in something like reading, studying or counseling, it was hard for him to relax and enjoy quietness or solitude. He'd always preferred hustle and bustle, people and activity.

I also tried to convince myself that part of our problem was that Don and I were total opposites and didn't know how to relate to one another. Being the solve-problems-as-soon-as-they-surface, take-charge type, if I screamed "Mouse!" I wanted somebody to kill it right then. But not Don. He was the unruffled, analytical sort who cautioned, "Wait.... Let's not kill it. It might be the neighbor's gerbil. Just leave it alone, and everything will work out. The little thing will be gone before you know it." It seemed that our ways of thinking were coming from just such opposite extremes about almost everything. On top of that, my family had always relied upon work as our outlet for stress. Don's family, on the other hand, had the attitude, "Take a break and forget it. Let's party!"

Then there was the indisputable fact that God had placed a special call upon Don's life. Because of Don's approachable, fathering-type gifting, persons were drawn to him for counsel and discipleship. I'd done enough counseling and discipling myself to know that such things take time. Yet, occasionally I sensed that the amount of time and attention my husband gave to a particular person was unhealthy. Because of a vacuum in Don's soul, the warmth and closeness that evolved from that one-on-one counseling relationship seemed to meet a deep need in his life. At least, that's the thought that kept coming to me as I fretted and prayed. I had no idea how right I was.

The Frightening Truth

As the lonely months dragged by, my husband grew quieter and even more withdrawn as the wall between us became higher and thicker. The gaps of unaccounted-for time in his schedule were causing arguments and tension between us. Finally, one night I was awakened by the sound of his deep, uncontrollable sobbing. Little by little, he blurted out the facts that filled in all the blanks in my mental list of questions and suspicions.

Don said he had been making trips into Seattle. But he had not been spending all those hours in the library or driving around to relax and clear his head, as he'd led me to believe. At first, he had begun yielding to a strangely compelling urge to browse through pornography in adult book stores. Then, as the impulse became more overpowering, he had visited a massage parlor. As a result, he had contracted a venereal disease. Certain that he had passed it on to me, Don had no choice but to tell me.

The next day, we drove to a health clinic in another city. We both felt the humiliation of giving assumed names before being tested and treated. Though the physical pain from several powerful injections I had to receive was severe, it in no way compared to the emotional pain of being forced up against a problem I had no clue on earth how to combat. In retrospect, even though it was a shaming, terrifying experience, at least it served for years as a deterrent to Don from acting out sexually in a manner that would endanger my health.

Tormented by what he had done, my husband knew he needed to find someone who could help him break free from the whirling cesspool threatening to drag him under.

Desperate and frightened, Don began visiting a psychiatrist. I was surprised when the psychiatrist asked to see me, but his counsel surprised me even more. "Mrs. Crossland," he said, "your husband has no choice about his bisexual behavior. You need to divorce him or accept him as he is."

Nowhere to Turn

I left the office that day shattered and stunned. What was I to do? I didn't know anyone in the ministry to go to, and I didn't want to cause people in the church to stumble. Members of my husband's family were beginning to turn to God, so I certainly did not want to damage their spiritual growth. Unable to talk with anyone about my pain and fears, I just bottled up everything inside and tried to live with it.

My husband never returned to that psychiatrist. Though Don and I occasionally made desperate attempts to reconnect in our spirits, now and then a deep sadness and heartbreaking heaviness inside me signaled that something was still very wrong.

The Unwelcome "Guest"

It was during that time that an invisible, but very real, stranger moved into our house. I could feel its dark, foreboding presence. I could sense the tentacles of its evil power tightening around my husband and around my heart, inserting doubts and fears into my mind. Plagued by jealousy, suspicion and a deepening sense of rejection, I gradually became very insecure, very isolated and very, very lonely.

Divine Interventions

During this dark, desperate time, God mercifully intervened in our lives. He placed us upon the heart of a Christian acquaintance, and she began praying about my problem with infertility.

One day the friend said, "Helen, God is going to give you and your husband a baby boy." Supposing she'd misunderstood the seriousness of my situation, I explained that the doctors had said I couldn't have any more children. Although I repeated exactly what the doctors had said to me, her faith remained undaunted. She assured me that we would have a son.

A few months after that conversation I became ill with what the doctor said was a horrible case of food poisoning. When I just couldn't seem to get over it, I went to another doctor who suggested I might have an ulcer and put me on a bland diet. Even then, I continued to feel absolutely awful. Supposing that the unusual sense of fatigue and listlessness accompanying my physical problems might be emotionally based, another doctor sent me to a psychiatrist. He finally admitted he couldn't help me, so I was sent to another physician. For 4 months I bounced from doctor to doctor until one of them finally said, "You're going to have a baby!"

When our son Rod was born, I couldn't wait to call the woman, now living overseas, who had by faith seen and foretold the miracle I was holding in my arms. All I said was, "Guess what has happened? I just had a baby!"

She laughed with delight and, without a moment's hesitation, asked, "What did you name him?" Him! Her faith had never wavered.

Soon afterward, we left our beloved congregation and Don accepted an invitation to work with a national seminar ministry. Before accepting his new position, Don shared with the leader about his inner struggles. Strangely, nothing was said in response, nor was it ever mentioned again. Occasionally, the leader would say there was one sin he did not know how to help people with. However, neither of us ever asked if he was referring to Don's sin.

Although the new job meant a lot of traveling for Don and some lonely times for me, our years with that ministry bought Don a welcomed reprieve. His isolated existence in Washington had bred addiction, but our move to Dallas and then Chicago, and Don's constant traveling put him in contact with pastors and other spiritual leaders all over the United States. He began flourishing spiritually as he built many healthy, solid relationships with godly men and women.

Losing Ground

Over a period of time, however, it became evident that restlessness and wandering were still very much a part of my husband's nature. It was as if he was always searching for something to fill a hole in his soul.

Through his work with the nationally respected ministry, Don was becoming better known. Invitations to pastor began coming in. Finally, weary of the emotional wear and tear involved in his years of travel and yearning to shepherd a congregation once again, Don accepted the call of a church in Waco, Texas, to become their senior pastor.

At the time we moved to Waco, Don and I had been married about 15 years. I had seen him make tremendously encouraging progress in the years since we had left Seattle. However, as Don stepped back into the role of esteemed spiritual leader, discipler and counselor, he began losing the spiritual ground he had fought to regain. Once again, building a big, successful church became his idol.

Our relationship began to slide. Now, more than ever, I sensed the evil shadow stalking our every step. I felt I had to always be on guard to maintain a protective vigil over Don and his whereabouts—not just for his sake, but for mine, as well. After all, my whole life revolved around him. I didn't know it, but I had an idol, too: my husband.

Since the day I'd married Don, I'd had no security or identity apart from what he provided. He had always been my life-source. Now that he was pulling away from me and relying upon his work and upon others to meet his needs, I felt as if I were dying.

Everything I did was geared to gain Don's approval and get his attention so he would meet my needs and I wouldn't have to be miserable inside. But in the end, instead of tying my husband to me, my desperate behaviors only pushed him further away.

The Death of a Dream

During that time Don's father became critically ill. Knowing that his dad was not a Christian, Don rushed to his bedside. He was given the opportunity to present God's plan of salvation and ask his father to accept Christ as his Savior. This time, the man who had always been so hardened and totally unresponsive to the Gospel, prayed with Don, asking Jesus to forgive his sins and become Lord of his life. My husband could hardly contain his joy and excitement. For the first time in his life, Don dared believe that the yawning emptiness in his soul might be filled with the acceptance, love and closeness he had unceasingly craved from his father.

But Don's lifelong dream was not to be fulfilled. The next morning during open heart surgery, his dad suffered a massive stroke that left him mentally incapacitated and unable to communicate. A short time later he developed cancer. Don continued to pray for his father's healing, desperately hoping that his dad would get better, but he died within a year.

Losing Brad had broken Don's heart. But losing his father and having to bury his life-long dream of having his dad's approval of his ministry caused the hole in Don's soul to erode until it became a chasm. Although something in Don still longed to break free and he continued to seek out help from counselors he felt he could trust, the story was always the same. Either the counselors lacked the divine insight and spiritual power to help him, or they eventually confessed that they, too, were entangled in sexual addiction.

All this time, I kept telling myself that if Don got okay, I would be okay, too. I didn't know it, but my need for help was as severe as my husband's.

Only a Matter of Time

I watched in despair as my husband began opening the door to "emotional adultery." I called it that because it seemed to me that all my husband's needs, even for conversation, were being met at church by people other than myself.

Before long, our relationship was practically non-existent. I recognized the familiar old behavior patterns emerging in my husband's life.... Staying at church or in his office until late at night. Avoiding intimacy with me. Becoming angry and defensive whenever I attempted to question or confront. Making up excuses to explain gaps of unaccounted-for time.

I seemed to live with a sinking, sick sensation in the pit of my stomach. The loneliness and feelings of rejection were almost unbearable. My emotional addiction was becoming life threatening. One day as Don started to leave the house, my desperation intensified. I felt I couldn't live if he drove away and left me alone again. Racing out the door in front of him, I threw myself down behind the back tires of the car. So what if someone passed by and saw my bizarre behavior? So what if a neighbor heard my hysterical screams? I couldn't have cared less. "If you leave, you'll have to run over me first!" I shrieked. "I'm not budging!"

Something Is Happening Inside....

Not long after that during another long, dreary night alone, I allowed the pain in my heart to pour out on paper:

6:45 P.M.—The loneliness is almost unbearable. The isolation is deafening. The pain of separation is excruciating. The sobs are pounding in my heart to escape. The circumstances are too similar. God, this is not life. This emotional prison is not the answer. I must hear from You.

8:30 P.M.—God, the silence of another evening alone is getting to me. I'm not single, so I can't go out with singles and be open. I can't share the many questions in my mind. Neither can I live in a "pretend" world. I am so lonely I really would prefer death. I must hear from You. You are my only trusted friend.

11:50 P.M.—Rod just came in and said, "Where's Dad? He's never home."

1:05 A.M.—Something is happening inside me....

When I wrote those last words I did not know what that

"something" was. I do now. Job put it into words for us thousands of years ago when he asked, "What strength have I left, that I should wait and hope? And what is ahead of me, that I should be patient?" (Job 6:11, Amp.).

Love, Hope and Faith had skipped merrily along beside me when Don and I first began our walk together. But the journey had been long and hard. Finally, the trail forked, and Don turned his back on me and walked away. Poisoned by anger and unforgiveness, the fragile love I'd felt for my husband gradually sickened and died.

Hope and Faith tried to continue the journey alone but were weak and powerless in themselves, for it is Love that bears all things, believes all things, hopes all things and endures all things, and Faith worketh by Love. Finally, Faith crumpled to the ground. Then Hope sank to its knees. It, too, was dying.

Anger and Rebellion crouched in the shadows. Watching.... Waiting.... Suddenly Hope pitched forward, face-down. At last! It had happened. Love, Faith and Hope were gone. Now Anger and Rebellion were in charge.

Vengeance Is Mine!

I was 95% certain that I was not imagining the suspicious circumstances surrounding my husband's behavior. Yet, like many other individuals married to mates trapped in sexual addiction, it was the remaining 5% shred of doubt, plus the desperate hope that God would answer my prayers and change my husband, that had always kept me holding on. But not any more. The carefully groomed woman with the empty eyes staring back at me from my mirror had endured all she intended to take of loneliness and rejection.

I'd prayed the same prayer for over 15 years, but nothing had changed— except for the worse. Well, God wouldn't have to put up with my useless prayers any more. I'd had enough! I was sick of hoping. Tired of waiting. I didn't intend to sit alone in an empty house any longer. My husband was never going to change.

All the lonely nights, all the unanswered prayers, all the seething anger and bitterness bottled up in my soul were finding vent at last, and it felt wonderful! Why on earth had I held on so long? Because I'd been a weak, stupid, naive little coward, that's why. But that was over. I was taking charge of my life!

My hardened, rebellious heart never flinched as I shook my fist at heaven and screamed out my ultimatum.... "I mean it, God! If Don gets involved with one more person, I will, too!"

The angry eyes in the mirror looked back at me with a silent stare of approval as if to say, "There! That will get His attention!"

I was too beside myself with rage to comprehend what was really happening, too rebellious to heed the Spirit's whispered warnings. All the years that Satan had invested in tormenting, discouraging and deceiving me had finally paid off. Now the Father of Lies was ready to move in for the kill....

Chapter 2

HE DID. I DID.

After Brad's death I'd become aware of an evil, invisible presence leering longingly at Don and me "through the windows" of our relationship. Next, I sensed that this unwelcome intruder had silently broken in and taken up residence in our home. At first, it had merely hovered in the background, but as time passed it grew bolder and began asserting itself.

Before I realized what was happening, the demonic presence had slunk out of its corner and was laying claim to more and more of the relationship Don and I enjoyed as husband and wife. Cutting off communication between us. Undermining our friendship. Shamelessly pushing its way in between us. Shutting off any affection.

Through the years of coexisting in the same house with an invisible enemy, I had grown familiar with its ways and tactics. I could even recognize similar spirits manipulating or controlling the lives of others, but I had no idea how to deal with such things. There was something else, too. It was as if some shadowy figure had forged an evil bond with Don somewhere in his past. Some dark memory, buried alive in a shallow grave within the recesses of my husband's being, stubbornly maintained a mystical grip on his will.

Sexual addiction now seemed to be in control of Don's life. I knew it was only a matter of time until he would allow another relationship to get out of hand. Yet I said no prayers. I felt no pity. Like vultures silently circling high in the sky above a wounded animal, Rage, Revenge and Contempt watched with unblinking stares. It would not be long now....

Walking Into the Trap

As strange as it may seem, I cannot recall how I discovered for sure that my husband was involved with someone else. The pain and the shame have simply erased the memory. But somehow I found out and when I did, my emotions careened absolutely out of control. God had failed me again!

I remember seething with anger as I mentally rehashed my torturing circumstances, justifying what I was about to do. "Here I sit like some isolated hermit, so lonely I could die, with no one to talk to, no one to understand what I'm going through. Well, enough is enough. If this is the way Don intends to live the rest of his life, then I can live my life that way, too."

If anyone had warned me five months before of the sordid mess in which I was about to become entangled, I would have recoiled in horror and disgust from the very mention of such a thing. But I had allowed bitterness and rebellion to erode my soul, and I had cast away my confidence in God. Now I was so empty, so starved for affection, so vulnerable, it wasn't hard to walk right into a trap.

I didn't have long to wait. As if on cue, another person began dropping flattering, not-so-subtle hints that he would love to give me the attention and affection I deserved.

Hardened and rebellious, I took great satisfaction in knowing that the same relationship which brought me pleasure could bring my unfaithful husband pain.

The first forbidden fruits were sweet and satisfying. The secrecy and seduction were exhilarating. I had finally found a way out of my loneliness. At last I had someone in my life who tenderly kissed me on the neck, said positive things to me and took time to talk and listen attentively. It was not hard to think I had fallen in love. I felt so alive, so free. Little did I realize that Satan has a false peace that feels so right...for a season.

Quicksand!

After a very few months of what I had considered to be my new-found freedom, guilt began eating me alive. What I was doing was wrong, and I knew it. No amount of rationalization or excuse-making could obliterate that fact.

Looking into the pure, trusting eyes of 15-year-old Tamra and 7-year-old Rod brought an avalanche of pain and regret. Teaching the women in my Sunday school class who had believed in and befriended me made me want to scream out, begging their forgiveness. Knowing that people struggling for survival were counting on me to pray and touch God for them caused me to cover my face in shame.

My brief season of pleasure had turned into torment. I felt hypocritical. Dirty. Unworthy to draw another breath. I knew I deserved to die. I was filled with such shame and self-hatred I could hardly look in the mirror. For the first time in my life, I realized that the pain of guilt and shame can be far worse than the pain of loneliness.

All excitement and fulfillment had drained out of my sordid relationship, but lacking the courage to break it off, I let it drag on. Finally, I realized that I had stepped into quicksand, and I could not get out.

Trapped!

When I went to the man and began trying to get out of the relationship, his passion changed to possessiveness. One time his words would be tender. The next, brutal. I felt trapped regardless of his response. Though he knew I longed to break free once and for all, he refused to leave me alone. I never had a moment's peace of mind. He was the stalker. I was the victim.

Finally, I could stand it no longer. Death would have been a blessed relief compared to the horror I was enduring. I had to break free. But how? Summoning every ounce of strength I possessed, once again I asked that he leave me alone. When I did, his flattering compliments and soft-spoken words of endearment turned into vicious threats.

At first, I was afraid he would expose our affair. Then, as his threats increased, my terror knew no bounds. "I think I'll kill you, Don and me," he whispered menacingly. "Imagine people driving in to work and seeing our bodies hanging from the Waco Bridge!"

Why? Why had I ever become involved with someone else? There was no telling what he might do now. Though I no longer had any desire to live, I had no desire to be murdered in cold blood, either.

My mind tiptoed back to the terror and confusion I'd felt when I was nine years old and found out that my grandmother's new husband, whom she had been so excited about marrying, had shot her, then turned the gun on himself. Several other murders had also occurred in my family through the years. I couldn't help wondering if my name was about to be added to that bloody list.

I was trapped in a pool of quicksand and it was dragging me under, sucking the very life out of me. If only there were someone I could trust. Someone with the wisdom and courage to help extricate me from my dilemma....

Unable to live with the torment any longer, I called a man on our church staff, Gary Smalley, who was also a dear friend. His wife, Norma was my best friend, and I felt safer with them than with anyone else. Afraid of being seen talking to anyone, I asked him to meet me in the parking lot of a local restaurant. As I sobbed out my shameful story, I could tell by the expression on his face that he was having a hard time believing everything he was hearing. After appearing speechless and in a state of shock for what seemed to be several minutes, he stammered out that he and his wife would stand with me and do everything in their power to help me. I can't remember for sure, but I think he also tried to reassure me of God's love and forgiveness and remind me that His merciful hand would be there to guide my future. I do recall breathing a shaky sigh of relief and thanking him for being there when I needed a friend so desperately.

As he walked back to his car and I drove away, my mind was occupied with other things.... From the time I was a little girl, I had yearned to be a woman of God and walk in His perfect will. Now, I felt that by entering into an affair I had forever forfeited my right to God's best. Not having God's best meant no hope, no future, no further reason to exist. I had sinned against God, against those who loved and believed in me and against those who would be caused to stumble if my sin ever came out into the open. Now, the kindest, most redemptive thing I could do for all of them was to make sure that I exited life as quickly and quietly as possible. That would be my next, and final, task....

Time to Say Goodbye

It was settled in my mind. I had no choice but to die. Piecing together my plan as I drove, I took the long way home, giving myself time to think through every detail.... First I would write a loving, reassuring letter to my children and family. Then I would take the pills from the medicine cabinet and lay down and die.

I was counting on an empty house and no interruptions but, to my dismay, Don was pacing the floor, waiting for me. My frantic thoughts darted here and there. Gary must have alerted him that he was needed at home. What else did he know? The moment I walked through the door, Don's searching gaze pinned me to the wall. "What is it?" he demanded nervously. "What's wrong?"

It was no use. Why should I hide it any longer? Woodenly, matter of factly, I told Don I'd been having an affair.

For an instant, Don reeled in shock. Then, like a caged animal backed in a corner and desperately fighting for life, my husband turned on me. Razor-sharp phrases from his verbal tirade clawed through my heart. "You! You of all people!" "...Always had you on a pedestal." "...Home so secure with you and the children...." "You betrayed me!"

Betrayed? Betrayed! How dare this man who had filled my life with years of unspeakable agony say such a thing to me? He didn't even know the meaning of the word.

Don grabbed me by the arm, pushing me toward the door. "Come on!" he ordered, his voice shaking. "We're confronting him right now!"

I don't remember the ride out into the country to the house where the person was staying, or what happened in those first moments after we arrived. I do remember demanding that I have a few minutes alone with him. I wanted to ask his forgiveness and attempt to clear my conscience. As I stammered out my apology, it was hard to admit that I had purposed to have an affair with him before he ever approached me. When I finished, he also asked me to forgive him. Now it was finally over. Done with. As I turned from him and walked away, my thoughts fixed on the only thing that would bring the release I craved: finding a way to die.

Then another car drove up. Gary and a medical doctor who attended our church stepped out. My thoughts began ricocheting wildly.

Why had he brought a doctor with him? He must have sensed what I was planning! I became hysterical. Nobody was going to stop me! Nobody!

"Calm down, Helen," I heard them saying in that soothing tone used for frightened, cornered animals. "Calm down.... Everything's going to be all right...."

I could not, I would not ever, ever, allow them to take me back into that lonely, meaningless world. I braced myself, waiting for the right moment....

In a sudden burst of strength I broke free from their grasp and bolted into the woods. Running at break-neck speed, I darted through the brush. I could hear someone behind me, closing in. Seconds later, it seemed that someone's body impacted with mine in a flying tackle, and strong arms clutched me in their grasp. Before I could scramble away, another set of arms locked around me.

I sobbed. I scratched and clawed. I struggled with all my might as Gary and one of his friends who was staying in the house where we were and the doctor strained to hold me. Finally, they picked me up bodily and carried me, kicking and screaming, to the car. Then they drove me to the hospital where the psychiatrist they had called was awaiting my arrival.

Waiting to Die

I have little, if any, recollection of the next few days. It was as if I released my grasp on the cord connecting me to life and reality, and my soul plunged downward into icy blackness. I do not know how deep into the dark pit of despair I sank, but at some point the last feeble ray of hope flickering far above me vanished. I learned later that the psychiatrist told Don that my depression was so deep it might require years of therapy, and even then I might never come out of it.

My desire to die was so overpowering it blotted out my maternal instincts. I don't even recall wondering how my children were doing. All I could manage to do in a 24-hour period, with the aid of a nurse's constant prodding, was brush my teeth one by one.

I welcomed the blankness, the numbness. And as soon as I had the opportunity, I would welcome death. I felt that the real me had died long ago, anyway. My physical death would be a mere formality, like disconnecting a body from life support.

Realizing that nothing the two of them were doing was making any difference in my condition, the doctor and psychiatrist decided that getting me away might help. The doctor talked his wife into taking me to their vacation home in Colorado. She didn't want to make the trip with me, and I didn't want to go. However, I cooperated when it dawned upon me that once I was out from under the protective surveillance of the hospital staff, it would be much easier to take my life.

On the day we were leaving for Colorado, the doctor's wife took a Guideposts magazine out of her mailbox and paused to thumb through it. "Hmmmm.... This is interesting," she said, pointing to an article mentioning a new book called My Friend, the Bible by John Sherrill. "He's talking about the necessity of feeding upon `manna' verses from the Bible every day. Isn't that good, Helen?" she asked, keeping up a friendly stream of surface chatter much like an attentive mother with a 2 year old. "When we get to Colorado, you and I are going to get a manna verse, a scripture that speaks to us personally, every day."

I nodded and sank back into foggy oblivion. I never intended to come back from Colorado. I was going there to die.

The Angel in Cowboy Boots

I don't recall much of the trip. I was in such depression, most of the time all I did was sleep. To this day I can't recall how the doctor's wife managed to get me to sit down at the roadside picnic she had prepared for the trip or how she persuaded me to go for a walk on a trail somewhere in New Mexico. What I do remember is how she held me like a child while I sobbed and screamed and moaned.

Sometime after we arrived and got settled, the doctor's wife secretly called a friend who lived nearby and asked her to come over and pray for me.

I was startled by a knock at the door. The person who strode into the room did not impress me. Her physical appearance did not fit my description of a godly woman. She said she had been taking care of her horses right before she came. I believed her. I could still smell their scent on her clothes.

Later, I learned that the woman had become a Christian a few years earlier and had been discipled by Agnes Sanford who authored a book on inner healing and deliverance called *The Healing Light.* God had begun a work in the woman from the inside out, the way it should be. To me, she didn't look like "Miss Christian" on the outside. However, I later discovered that she loved Jesus and was growing into a powerful woman of God. As a matter of fact, she was so open and receptive to the changes God was bringing about in her life that she said she now bought only one pack of cigarettes at a time. "I know I won't be smoking forever," she explained with a faith-filled smile.

But I didn't know any of that when she tromped across the room and pulled up a chair beside me. Repulsed by the smell of cigarette smoke, her rough exterior and tough manner, I just wished she would stomp back out the door and leave me alone. Instead, she looked me straight in the eyes and asked, "Do you want to be this way the rest of your life?"

I stared back, too weary to reply. I don't even want a "rest of my life," I thought to myself. But if I'm going to have a rest of this life, no, I don't want to be like this.

Ignoring my silence, the woman continued. "God has given me a ministry of praying for people in depression. I believe the Lord has told me to come and pray for you. You can lay right where you are and go to sleep, if you like. It doesn't matter. I just want to be obedient to the Lord."

She closed her eyes and began to pray. I took her up on her offer, shut my eyes and drifted back into the fog. Right before falling asleep, I remember hearing her praying something about my life being like a stopped-up river and asking God to begin clearing out the debris so the waters could flow again.

There is no explanation for what happened, other than God's love and mercy and a woman's faith, prayers and obedience.... But when I awoke, the black night of depression was fading, and hope was dawning. It was as if something had reversed. For the first time in months, life was flowing into me instead of ebbing out. I had energy. Something in me wanted to get out of bed. Perhaps.... Perhaps, it even wanted to live....

Finding the Way Back

After that breakthrough, the doctor's wife began reading 5 psalms to me every morning. Without fail, God supplied a 'manna' verse that ministered to me so strongly, I had no doubt that the Lord knew exactly where I was and that He was speaking those words directly to me. It was as if He was depositing little golden nuggets of hope in my bankrupt spirit.

Some of those manna verses became desperate prayers expressing the depth of my needs:

"Arise, O Lord, O God, lift up Thy hand. Do not forget the afflicted" (Ps. 10:12, NAS).

"Search me, O God, and know my heart" (Ps. 139:23).

"Do not incline my heart to any evil thing, to practice deeds of wickedness with men who do iniquity..." (Ps. 141:4).

"Teach me the way in which I should walk; for to Thee I lift up my soul" (Ps. 143:8).

Other manna verses became a lifeline of hope for the days ahead:

"In the morning, O Lord, Thou wilt hear my voice; in the morning I will order my prayer to Thee and eagerly watch" (Ps. 5:3).

"The Lord also will be a stronghold for the oppressed; a stronghold in time of trouble" (Ps. 9:9).

"The Lord is near to the brokenhearted, and saves those who are crushed in spirit" (Ps. 34:18).

"For thou hast rescued my soul from death, my eyes from tears, my feet from stumbling. I shall walk before the Lord in the land of the living" (Ps. 116:8,9).

One morning just as I awoke, I sensed the Lord speaking inaudibly, yet clearly, deep inside me. "Helen, if you will let Me, I will teach you about My peace and My rest and My joy. But you must be willing to take your eyes off your husband and everything else that is happening around you."

Peace? Rest? Joy? Did they really exist? Was God offering them to me? Was He about to change Don? When I got back to Waco, were things going to be different?

I closed my eyes and let the grateful tears spill down my cheeks. "I will let You, Lord," I whispered. "I will let You. Please teach me. I don't know how to go about it, but I'm ready to start rebuilding my life."

Thanks to two faithful Christian women who had taken time to pour the cleansing wine and healing oil of the Spirit into my wounded heart and bind up my broken spirit, and to those others who were praying for me, my journey toward wholeness had begun. The time had come for me to go home.

Chapter 3

SINKING SAND OR SOLID ROCK?

Hoping that my husband would be changed when I returned home, I noticed immediately that his outward behavior was different. Don made an all-out effort to do the right things and say the right words. We attended a couples group that focused on accountability, especially the husband's. He and I read scripture and prayed together every morning. Yet, even though he and others assured me that his addiction was now a thing of the past, I knew immediately that the evil, invisible presence was still in our home. I squared my shoulders and tried to prepare myself for the long haul.

Mercifully, at that point, I didn't have the slightest inkling that my husband's emotional and sexual addiction would steadily worsen over the next seven years. Neither did I know that I had the same amount of time to be rebuilt from the inside out before a trauma of proportions I'd never imagined unleashed its fury.

Coping With Reality

When I first returned home, I felt too fragile emotionally to shoulder my role as a wife. It may not have been a mentally healthy thing to do, but for a few weeks the only way I knew how to cope was by taking off my wedding rings and pretending to myself that I was just a maid and nanny working in the home. That way, I could keep the household running fairly well and see that the children were cared for without being torn apart by my loneliness and the lack of love between Don and me.

My self-chosen job description included grocery shopping, cooking, doing laundry, cleaning house, working in the yard and taking care of Tamra and Rod. It also included sleeping on my side of the bed in our master bedroom. Our sex life had become practically non-existent, so I didn't feel too threatened there. Crawling into bed so I could drop off to sleep was simply the last item I checked off on my mental "things-to-do" list each day.

Plugging Back Into Life

Pretending to be a maid and nanny might work for a little while, but I knew I couldn't live the rest of my life avoiding reality, pressures and problems. "Lord," I prayed, "I'm ready to let You teach me about Your peace, rest and joy. I'm willing to take my eyes off my husband and everything happening around me. I just don't know how. Unless You take my hand and lead me, I'm not going to make it. Lord, do whatever You have to do. Teach me Your ways. Show me Your paths. I want to be a whole, healthy person according to Your standards, not mine."

When I uttered those words, I did not know that some of my most basic beliefs were flawed. I had no idea that I was a slave to my feelings. I did not know that I could not change my feelings until I changed my beliefs.... But God knew. I had asked Him to help me, and He was about to answer.

Choosing The Right Focus

Soon after praying that prayer, I went to see a person I'd met earlier who did counseling in her office at home. That day her heart seemed to overflow with wisdom for me. I hoped she could share something that would help me understand how to obey God's instructions to take my eyes off my husband and everything around me. Sure enough, the counselor gave me exactly the help I needed.

She told me to imagine that the room in which we were sitting represented the inside of me and to pretend that the room's only furnishings were a couch and a chair. "Now," she continued, "if this room is the inside of you, everyone and everything else in your life is outside the door. Is that correct?"

I nodded.

"Just to make sure it's clear," she said, "let me say that another way. If the room is inside you, no person or circumstances can get past that door and into the room. Right?"

I nodded once more. Now that I had mentally separated the inside of myself from everybody and everything going on around me, I was ready to hear what she said next.

My friend continued. "Now, you get to decide where you stay in this room—on the couch or in the chair."

The fact that I could make a choice was an interesting concept to me. For so long I'd felt as if I were being carried down the rapids of a rushing river and had neither oars nor a life jacket. If I really did have a choice, maybe the promise of peace, rest and joy could become a reality after all.

"First, let's talk about the couch in this room inside you," my friend said. "That is where you have spent your life. You see, when you're on the couch, you are looking horizontally at the people and circumstances outside the door and believing that they are 'causing' you to be where you are."

I nodded, realizing that I was focused on people and circumstances, constantly looking at my husband and people he was with and blaming them for my misery.

My friend continued her analogy. "On the couch is where you say, 'You make me so angry.' 'It's all your fault that I'm depressed.' 'If you would pay attention to me, I would be happy.' On the couch, you feel victimized by the people and circumstances in your life and believe they have to change before you can be happy or have any peace. On the couch, fear, anger and all the other unhealthy emotions can attack you. It's a miserable place to be."

I understood what she was saying. My friend was describing my feelings exactly.

"If you believe you're on the couch because of people or circumstances outside the door of your inner life, you will either consciously or subconciously attempt to manipulate, control or change those people or circumstances. But that's impossible to actually accomplish. You'll wind up exhausted, frustrated and depressed.

I knew that what she was saying was true. I'd been there, and it was a dangerous place to be.

"Helen," she said, "now I want you to picture yourself in that same room, but this time instead of lying helplessly on the couch, you're sitting upright in a chair. You're no longer allowing circumstances to dictate your feelings or responses. You're not depending on people or on what's going on around you to make you feel happy and fulfilled.

"When you're sitting in the chair, you're still well aware of what is happening outside your door, but you're choosing a vertical focus rather than the familiar horizontal one," she continued. "By maintaining an upward focus on the Lord and hearing what He is saying, you can remain joyful and peaceful in spite of what's going on around you. However, anytime you choose to do so, you can revert to the horizontal focus on people and problems, lie down on the couch and forfeit your rest, joy and peace of mind.

"Helen, when you're sitting in the chair," she concluded, "you're depending upon the Holy Spirit to strengthen you. You're choosing to base your thoughts, words and feelings upon the Word of God. You're living for God's glory. And you are trusting Him to perfect everything that concerns you." She paused. "Does what I've said make any sense at all?" "Yes.... Yes, it does," I assured her, deep in thought. By using the example of the room, couch and chair this person couldn't have described my situation any better if she'd drawn me a picture and colored it.

Sand Or Rock?

After our conversation, I thought a lot about the principles that had been shared with me. I knew what the counselor had told me was scriptural. Her illustration reminded me of the parable of the two builders that Jesus shared in Matthew 7:24-27. To me, the wise man who built his house—his life— upon the rock and saw it standing strong in the midst of the storm was like the person who chose to sit in the chair, focusing on God and hearing His voice. When the storms came, his life didn't fall apart because he had built it upon the strong foundation of Christ Himself. The foolish man who did not act upon the truth, but built his house—his life— upon the sand, was like the person lying on the couch, blaming people and circumstances. When the rain and the floods came and the winds blew against his house, it collapsed.

Though I'd studied and taught the Bible, I had not built my life upon the rock by trusting God, hearing His Word and acting upon it. Instead, I had built my life on sand.... Fallible people. Shifting emotions. Ever-changing circumstances. Faulty beliefs. No wonder my life had come tumbling down.

False Peace Versis God's Peace

I had focused on my husband, people and circumstances and believed they were causing my misery, restlessness and lack of peace. As a result of my efforts to manipulate and control people and situations, I sometimes saw a little improvement. At that point, my emotions calmed down and I experienced a false peace, resulting in temporary relief..

The more I thought about that false peace, the more I realized that it was like standing on a beach where the sand felt as hard as a rock under my feet...until a wave came rolling in. Suddenly that rock-hard sand began to feel like quicksand. My times of false, temporary peace based upon a temporary solution could dissolve just that quickly. Suddenly, my misery turned into a feeling of helplessness. Helplessness led to hopelessness. Then came depression and the thought, "Why should I even keep on living? Nothing seems to be changing."

I began to understand that unlike a false, temporary peace, God's peace was a permanent solution. It would not dissolve or let me down during times of crisis or change.

Deception

John 10:10 says that "the thief comes only to steal, and kill, and destroy." One of the ways that Satan had stolen from me was by deception. Knowing that the earlier in life he can lure us into deception the easier it will be to keep us there, Satan had begun deceiving me with his lies while I was very young.

The deception that others were "causing" me to be unhappy grew from seeds planted in my mind as a child through statements I'd overheard from people I loved, respected and trusted. "If only my husband would stop drinking I could have some peace." "If only my husband would stop looking at other women I could have rest." "If my child would stop rebelling and start serving God I could be happy." "If only I had a better job and could move to a better place I...." "If only I weren't single...." "If I could have a baby...." "If I were smarter...." If.... If.... If....

My life with Don had been built upon "if only's." If only he loved me with all his heart I could be happy. If only I could trust him I could have peace. If only I weren't so lonely I wouldn't feel so depressed and miserable. If only Don would change I wouldn't have to walk in fear, rejection and insecurity. Yet all my efforts to manipulate, control or change my husband had failed. I was a helpless victim.

I was beginning to realize that my husband, not God had been my focus. I had made Don, not God, my life source. I'd thought that everything most important to me depended upon what Don did or did not do: Our children's welfare. My peace and happiness. My fulfillment and future. My security and reputation. That's why I'd prayed for years, "God, please change my husband."

Building On The Rock

Comparing the counselor's example of sitting in the chair with the scriptural principle of building upon the rock, I realized that I must make Christ Himself—not feelings—the foundation upon which I lived and built my life. On the rock, the really important thing was to hear God and have an obedient heart toward Him. Then my focus immediately would go, like a vertical line, straight to the heart of my Father God. Then I could pray, "God, can't you see what is happening. You are the only one who sees and knows the overall picture. What do You want me to do or say?"

On the rock, where God's grace resides, I could feel secure even in the midst of all the stormy chaos and turmoil going on around me. I could be protected by abiding in the shadow of the Almighty, in the shelter of the Most High. I could say of the Lord, "He is my refuge and my fortress, my God in whom I trust" (Ps. 91:2).

On the rock, I could believe and receive Christ's promise, "Peace I leave with you; My peace I give to you..." (Jn. 14:27). I could receive

His rest for my soul (Matt. 11:28-30). On the rock, my joy would be made full (Jn. 15:11). The peace, rest and joy that He promised to give would be dependent upon where I was with Him, not upon anyone or anything around me. Just the thought of really being able to have His peace, rest and joy regardless of my circumstances gave me a hope I had never experienced.

Living In The Answers

I had been living in the problem, not in the answer. Now I was beginning to understand. I had options. I had choices. I could choose to live on the sand and be a victim, or I could choose to live on the rock and be a victor. I could choose to focus on people and things—making them my life source—and live in turmoil, torment and fear because of what was going on around me. Or, I could choose to focus on the Lord—making Him my life source and choosing to trust His promises—and experience His peace, rest and joy regardless of my circumstances.

What The Bible Says

As I studied what the Word of God has to say about His peace, rest and joy, it sounded too good to be true. When I build my life on the rock, He causes all things (regardless of how bad those things might be) to work together for my good (Rom. 8:28). On the rock, even evil can be overcome with good (Rom. 12:21). On the rock, if I seek first His kingdom and righteousness, all the things I need shall be added to me (Matt. 6:33).

Peace

As I studied the Scriptures I discovered that Jesus doesn't promise, "Peace I leave with you if your circumstances improve... My peace I give to you if your mate or child changes." No, He says, "Peace I leave with you, My peace I give to you; not as the world gives do I give to you. Let not your heart be troubled, neither let it be afraid" (Jn. 14:27). Obviously, you and I have a choice in the matter.

Paul declares that he learned to be content. That is, by use and practice, he acquired the habit of being content—satisfied to the point where he was not disturbed or disquieted—in whatever state he was. He says that he had learned, in any and all circumstances, the secret of facing every situation. "I have strength for all things in Christ Who empowers me—I am ready for anything and equal to anything through Him Who infuses inner strength into me, [that is, I am self-sufficient in Christ's sufficiency]." (See Phil. 11-13, Amp.)

Rest

What about God's rest? As I meditated upon the familiar words of Jesus in Matthew 11:28-30, they took on a deeper meaning. "Come to Me, all who are weary and heavy-laden, and I will give you rest. Take My yoke upon you, and learn from Me, for I am gentle and humble in heart; and you shall find rest for your souls. For My yoke is easy, and My load is light" (Matt. 11:28-30, NKJV). Studying it out word by word, I discovered that the rest Jesus offers us isn't dependent upon anyone or anything other than our own relationship with Him, our obedience to Him and our learning of Him.

Jesus invites the laboring, the heavy-laden, the over-burdened to come to Him. To take His useful, comfortable, pleasant yoke upon us and be coupled together with Him, actually sharing the yoke. To bear His light, easily borne burden. To learn, ever increasing in knowledge of Him who is gentle and humble in heart—a process not merely of getting to know Him but of applying that knowledge and walking differently. The result? We will find relief, refreshment and blessed quiet for our soul.

Joy

What about God's joy? In my study I learned that in both the Old and New Testaments, God Himself is the basis and object of the Christian's joy. Contrary to our human reasoning, persecution for Christ's sake enhances joy. Experiences of sorrow actually enlarge our capacity for joy. Paul writes it down for us in black and white:

Moreover—let us also be full of joy now! Let us exult and triumph in our troubles and rejoice in our sufferings, knowing that pressure and affliction and hardship produce patient and unswerving endurance.

And endurance (fortitude) develops maturity of character—that is, approved faith and tried integrity. And character [of this sort] produces [the habit of] joyful and confident hope of eternal salvation (Rom. 5:3,4, Amp.).

If you and I practice what we learn from the Scriptures, if we model our way of living upon those truths, the God of peace—of untroubled, undisturbed well-being—will be with us. (Phil. 4:9, Amp.)

Choosing The Right Response

Only a day or so after I'd seen the counselor, the Lord used my son to reveal another truth critical to my task of rebuilding. Returning from the grocery store, I parked the car in our driveway and opened the door to get out. At that moment, a snake almost six feet long slithered out from under the car. It was the biggest snake I'd ever seen outside a zoo. Screaming loudly enough to raise the dead, I ran to get a heavy garden rake propped against the corner of the house so I could kill the horrible creature.

Just then, Rod came running around the side of the house to see what all the commotion was about. His concern for me evaporated when he saw the long, scaly reptile gliding across the concrete. "Look, Mom!" my "Ranger Rick" son exclaimed in delight. "It's a snake!"

Rod had always been the adventurous type. More times than I cared to recall I'd caught him playing with little garter snakes. Suddenly, before I could stop him, he grabbed the huge snake just behind its head and began draping its coils over his shoulders.

"Rod, put that snake down," I shrieked. "It will bite you and you'll die! Put it down this instant!"

"Oh, Mom," he groaned in that disgusted tone of voice that boys reserve for sissies and over-protective mothers. "It's just a friendly little thing . It's not poisonous. Look at the shape of its pupils. They're round. And see its jaws? They're not square like those of a poisonous snake. There's nothing to be afraid of, Mom. Snakes are one of God's gifts to us."

I backed up, well out of reach. I had no intention of getting close enough to check out the creature's pupils. A shudder ran down my spine. Gift or no gift, I didn't want anything to do with it.

For the next two hours Rod went up and down the street, showing all the kids what he'd found. He entertained the whole neighborhood with that snake. When he got through, Rod put the thing down in the grass and said, "Okay, now you can go on and visit your family. Thanks for playing with me."

As I watched in amazement, it was as if I sensed God saying, "That snake didn't make you upset, and the snake didn't make Rod happy and excited. You simply responded according to the way you feel about snakes, and Rod responded according to the way he feels."

The more I reflected on what the Lord had shown me, the more I realized that this truth also applied to other emotions, such as anger and sadness. For example, I'd always believed that other people had the power to make me angry or sad. How many times had I thought, "You make me so angry," or "That makes me so sad," or, "What that person said really upset me" ?

Surface causes and shallow thinking had been a normal part of life as I lived on the sand, controlled by feelings, circumstances and people. But now, a second principle for rebuilding my life on the rock was forming in my mind: People and circumstances are not what make me angry, sad, happy or fearful. My anger, sadness, happiness and fear come from things deep inside me.

I can blame people or circumstances and try to make them responsible for my reactions. I can pour my time and energy into useless efforts to control, manipulate and change other people and, by doing so, allow them and their behaviors to control me. Or I can face the fact that I cannot change others: I can only change my responses to them. I can take reponsibility for what I do have power and control over—myself. I can give up trying to control others and allow them to take responsibility for their own behaviors and the consequences.

As I watched that 5-feet-11-inch (Rod had actually gotten the tape measure out to see how long his "friend" was) snake go slithering off into the weeds that day, I still had little appreciation for him or for reptiles of any description. But how very, very much I appreciated the divinely arranged lesson that the slithery creature and my son had illustrated before my eyes.

Living By The Book

Within a matter of days, I was forced to begin practicing the principles I'd discovered regarding God's peace, rest and joy and choosing righteous responses.

The person with whom I'd had the affair began to harass us. Once again, he threatened to murder us. He got drunk and drove up and down our street, back and forth in front of our house. One night he bashed in our mailbox in a fit of rage. Another night he came over drunk and laid on our sidewalk for over an hour, refusing to move and yelling obscenities all the while. Mercifully, our neighbors seemed totally oblivious to him and his strange behaviors. I breathed a very grateful prayer when his rage was finally spent and he gave up and left us alone.

Kicking The Habit

Even though God was teaching me how to live my life on the rock, it didn't take me long to recognize that it was one thing to know the right thing to do, but it was quite another thing to actually choose to do it. I hadn't realized just how much I'd come to relish the false comfort I'd derived from saying, thinking and doing the wrong things. Harboring anger and bitterness and wallowing in self-pity. Blaming others and bemoaning my circumstances. Playing the role of a helpless victim. Suddenly, all those things had become "no-no's." Now I knew that I — not my circumstances or someone else—was responsible for my own thoughts, feelings and actions.

At first, I neither wanted nor liked that responsibility, but it was mine just the same. I might as well accept it. If I were to ever be whole, many of my deeply engrained habit patterns had to be broken.

Learning To Build On The Rock

The next three years of my life were especially tough. I continually wrestled to overcome the destructive habit patterns that had propelled me to the brink of suicide. Yet while I was struggling, my husband was sinking deeper and deeper.

Don's addiction was so out of control I'm almost certain that I could have caught him if I'd chosen to play "detective" and been persistent. As a matter of fact, I'd had that very intent on several occasions during those first three years when, overcome by fear and anger, I took matters into my own hands. However, I never did catch him, and Don always denied any sexual involvement when I angrily confronted him.

It's not that the confronting, in itself, was wrong. Confrontation, in the right way and for the right reasons, is an act of love, for we are fulfilling our responsibility to (not for) someone by confronting evil when we see it and setting the necessary limits. However, because I didn't know how to go about confronting, my faulty methods and impure motives backfired. I'd stand there with nothing but anger and accusations while Don fabricated logical, legitimate-sounding excuses and accused me of being jealous and suspicious. Then I'd walk away wondering if maybe the problem really was that I was just jealous and suspicious—or crazy!

It's one thing to confront by screaming, "Why do you keep acting like this? It's ruining you and your ministry, it's ruining our home and it's making me hate you. How can you do this to your family? What's wrong with you anyway?"

It's quite another to calmly, but firmly, say, "I realize I cannot choose for you what you do, who you see, or how you spend your time. You have to hear God for yourself and decide whether or not you will obey what He says. I have made the choice to hear and obey Him, and I believe He has told me that I cannot walk with you in this direction."

As I struggled with these issues God convicted my heart, showing me that in the past I had perverted the word "submission." I had thought that if I obeyed my husband, I was obeying God. But God spoke these words firmly to my spirit: "You shall have no other gods before Me!" Without realizing what I was doing, I had set up my husband as a god in my life. God helped me recognize my error and embrace the truth. I was to respect Don as my husband, recognize his place of leadership in our home and walk in a spirit of submission, but I was not to make him my Lord and Master or look to him as my life-source. I, too, had a reponsibility to hear and obey God. If what Don wanted me to do and what God wanted me to do conflicted, I must obey God.

During that time, my Christian "walk" was more like a roller coaster ride. One day I'd bask in the rest, peace and joy that came from dwelling up on the rock. The next, I'd indulge in rage and self-pity, focus on the latest gut-wrenching chain of events, or try to manipulate or control a situation, and down I'd fall into the sand.

Every time I fell, it was as if God placed His hand on my shoulder and whispered gently, "Helen, you can stay in the sand, and I'll keep right on loving you. But if you really want Me to teach you, you'll have to let go of this thing and trust Me to take care of it for you."

My "God Bag"

For years, Satan had used worry and fear to torment me during those endless, anxious hours when Don was nowhere to be found. "Do you know what he's doing?" "Do you know who he's with?" "What if he contracts some horrible disease and passes it on to you?" "What if he gets caught with someone? What will happen to the disillusioned young Christians and disappointed believers who trusted him? What will happen to your own children when they find out that their daddy—their pastor—has been involved in sexual perversion?"

They were legitimate questions. Facts I had to acknowledge. Frightening possibilities I had to face. But I could not allow fear to torment and dominate me, driving me back to hopelessness and despair. How was I supposed to handle it all?

About that time I happened to read about someone who had made a "God bag" to help them deal with tormenting worries and fears. I decided to borrow the idea and see if it would work for me. I got a plain old brown paper sandwich bag, wrote "God Bag" on the outside and placed it in the safest, most private place I could find—the bottom of my lingerie drawer. When Satan bombarded my mind with fears and disturbing circumstances, I'd grab a 3-by-5 card and jot down my fear or worry. Then I'd say, "Okay, Satan, I am committing this to God. He is the One who can take care of it, not me. Watch me while I put this card into my bag. The moment it goes in, the fear and the entire situation are under the blood of Jesus, and I will have nothing further to do with them."

I wasn't trying to deny the problems. I knew they were real:

life-and-death real. But I also knew I could neither control nor handle them on my own.

I wasn't suppressing my feelings, either. Although I didn't know how to put it into words, I knew that my "negative" emotions such as fear, anger and sadness were counterfeits of the positive gifts God had given to serve me in legitimate functions. Sadness, for example, drained me, but godly sorrow told me I had lost something and allowed for healthy grieving that resulted in healing and strength. Fear said, "Move away! Withdraw! Be careful!" Faith said,"God, what do you want me to do or say?" Anger told me I was in danger of being controlled or injured. Boldness lovingly protected my boundaries from being violated.

I respected and readily acknowledged my emotions, but I knew from past experience that if I did not take control of my feelings—even legitimate feelings—they would take control of me.

Teacher Or Student?

A friend of mine used an illustration that helped put the whole issue of feelings into the proper perspective for me. "Feelings," she explained, are to be your students, and you are to be their teacher. You are responsible for their training and discipline."

The Holy Spirit later gave me an even more precise word regarding feelings. He showed me that my feelings were a part of my soul and that my soul was designed to be under the control of my spirit, where the Spirit of God resides with His wisdom. My body could not discern, in itself, which it was to obey—my soul, or my spirit. It simply obeyed the stronger of the two. Whether my soul or my spirit was stronger was determined by which one I fed and nourished the most and allowed to be in charge.

In the past, instead of nourishing my spirit (the teacher) by hiding God's Word in my heart and meditating upon it night and day, I had worried, meditating on my problems. I had not allowed my spirit to be in control of my feelings (the students) so they could be disciplined and trained. Instead, I had fed my feelings the most by giving in to their demands, indulging their fleshly appetites and letting them have their way.

Both my feelings and my spirit needed to be nourished and cared for, but I had neglected my spirit and overfed my feelings. Consequently, while my spirit was being deprived and weakened, my feelings were becoming "fat slobs" who acted and behaved very irresponsibly.

God never intended for my mind to be conformed to the thinking and customs of the world around me. He desired for me to be transformed—changed through a process of growth just as a caterpillar is gradually transformed into a butterfly. How? First, by renewing my mind— by willingly adjusting my thinking, ideals and attitudes to the mind of God revealed in His Word. Second, by trying to discern and approve what was good and acceptable and perfect in God's sight for me. (See Rom. 12:2.)

Instead of conforming my mind, will and emotions to the Word of God and being transformed by the renewing of my mind, for years I had permitted my feelings (the students) to make the decisions for my life and assume the place of authority. All the while, my spirit patiently and lovingly followed along, attempting in its weakened state to get my attention. "You're headed for dangers that you can avoid if you will allow me to be in my rightful place of authority," my spirit pled. But deceived by my strong, overpowering feelings, I ignored my spirit's urging. As a result, the students (my spiritually immature and irresponsible feelings) almost burned down the "school house."

Changing And Rearranging

I well remember the day I chose to allow my spirit to assume its rightful place of leadership. It didn't take long for an occasion to arise where my feelings were accustomed to being in control. But this time, I was prepared.

I knew that a wise leader is one who doesn't try to prove his authority. He knows exactly where he is supposed to go, and he recognizes and respects the obstacles. Instead of retreating in fear, he advances in faith. Therefore, even though I felt a little awkward, I said aloud, "Feelings, I realize you have been allowed to be in charge. However, that is not the way God designed it to be. Therefore, I will let my spirit make this decision, and that's the way we will go."

My feelings immediately threw a spoiled fit. They liked the position they'd had all those years and were unwilling to submit to my spirit. Rather than giving in to them, I repeated, "Feelings, I know this is very hard for you, but I love you enough to allow you to hurt a while in order that you may be healed and made whole."

After that, my spirit heard and responded to the Spirit of God within, and my body, through my will, obeyed. My feelings didn't want to go along, so they kept running off in different directions and trying every way they could to get back in control. But in spite of their rebellion and stubbornness, my spirit responded to them gently and tenderly instead of becoming abusive or harsh. It recognized that they were having a hard time relinquishing control. My spirit let my feelings know that it understood, but it also let them know that if I was ever going to become a healthy, whole person my mind, will, and emotions would all have to work together in submission to the Spirit of God Himself.

My spirit began limiting and redirecting my will, and teaching my mind, all the while leaving my emotions no doubt as to who was in control. Over the next months as I utilized my "God Bag" to help me practice this healthy self-discipline, my feelings began to stop pulling and tugging in opposite directions whenever my spirit made a decision. As my feelings gradually began submitting to my spirit they became restful and peaceful—even joyful.

There'll Be Some Changes Made

By that time in my life, I had progressed to the point where I finally understood that I could neither change my husband nor control him. I could pray for him. I could confront him in the right way whenever the opportunity arose. But I could not dictate who Don saw, where he went, or what he did.

I had finally arrived at the truth that the only person I could change (by the help and grace of God) was myself. Wouldn't you know it? God already had me signed up for that very course in His school of the Spirit.

Chapter 4

BUILDING UP AND TEARING DOWN

I'd always enjoyed certain books on our children's bookshelves. One evening I picked up one of my favorites, All Wrong Mrs. Bear, and began to read:

Mrs. Bear was a cross old thing. She was never very happy. She was always frowning and growling and snarling. She was unhappy because of the way she looked. Her thick, brown fur was too heavy. Her teeth were too big. Her claws were too long and frightening.

"I'm made all wrong," she growled to herself, as she went grumbling along through the forest. As she was walking, she met Robert Rabbit coming up out of his house-in-the-ground.

"Hrumpf!" growled Mrs. Bear. "Just look at you. You're made all wrong. you are so little that you can't fight for yourself. You have to live in a house-in-the-ground where it's dark and cold."

Robert Rabbit just smiled. "Good morning Mrs. Bear," he said. "I'm very glad to be a rabbit. I'm so little that I can hide almost anywhere. I live in a house-in-the-ground so the dogs can't find me. For me, it's a fine house. Besides, Mrs. Bear, didn't you know? God made me the way I am, and God does everything right."[1]

Somewhere about there in the story, I stopped reading that little children's book, and it started reading me. As Mrs. Bear stomped through the forest, meeting Mr. Rabbit, Billy Frog and Orville Owl, and the same basic scenario was repeated, my heart sat up and paid attention.

---

[1]Catherine Runyon, *All Wrong Mrs. Bear*, exerpted from pp. 5-10.

Finally, Mrs. Bear began to cry because she was made all wrong and nobody wanted to be her friend. Robert Rabbit, Billy Frog and Orville Owl heard her weeping and rushed to her aid. As the little animals expressed their concern and affection for her, Mrs. Bear stopped crying and asked:

"Would you really like to be my friends? Even if I'm made all wrong?"

"You're not all wrong, Mrs. Bear," said Robert Rabbit. "God gave you those big teeth to scare away hunters."

"And God gave you those big paws and claws so that you could get the honey out of bee trees," said Billy Frog.

"And God gave you a thick coat of fur to keep you warm all winter long while you sleep," said Orville Owl.

"And besides, Mrs. Bear," said all the animals together, "didn't you
know—"

"Yes, I know," said Mrs. Bear with a happy smile. "God made me the way I am, and God does everything right."

Long after I had closed the little book and slipped it back into its familiar spot on the bookshelf, Mrs. Bear's words rang in my ears: "God made me the way I am, and God does everything right...." Through a simple story for little children, the Lord was speaking to me once again about matters He desired to help me address: my low sense of self-worth and lack of identity.

I had never accepted myself. I'd always felt ugly. Deep in my heart, I thought that God had made many mistakes when He made me.

And then there was this thing of identity. Self-image. Self-esteem. Self-respect. If you asked me, they all sounded self-centered and unspiritual. Yet I had to admit that I didn't have a clue who I was apart from being Don's wife. I'd never given much consideration to my own individuality or separateness apart from my birth family or from my husband. I had married so young, I'd simply gone from thinking of myself as my parent's daughter to seeing myself as the pastor's wife.

In the small church in which I had grown up, childrens' and teenagers' Sunday school classes were divided into the categories of

Beginners, Primaries, Intermediates and Young People. To be promoted from Intermediates to Young People, a teenager had to be 17 by April 1. That left me out because I wasn't 17 until May. As a result, I had the dubious distinction of being promoted directly from the Intermediate department into the position of pastor's wife.

It goes without saying that I was completely overwhelmed by the role into which I'd been thrust. No matter how hard I tried, I felt totally inadequate for such a job. It wasn't that I was afraid of work. My dad farmed hundreds of acres of land, most of them owned by a wealthy Texas family. My sister and brothers and I had worked in the cotton fields for our father since we were children. As soon as the cotton started coming up around May, we'd be in the fields after school. Wearing hats or bonnets and long-sleeved shirts to keep from getting sunburned, we'd walk up one row and down another, hoeing weeds and pesky Johnson grass for hours on end. Because my dad had been made to carry heavy responsibilities at a very young age, he viewed the times when other kids would be off playing and having fun as opportunities for us to catch up on more work.

I thought nothing of being sent out to a field to move miles (or so it seemed to me) of irrigation pipe. The pipe, 4 or more inches in diameter, was connected in 10 to 12-foot sections. Sinking up to our knees in mud, my brother and I would unhook one section of the pipe at a time, straining to lift one end so all the water could run out. Then we would pick up the section of pipe, trudge 12 or more rows over, push one end of that section into the end of the last, then hook the two pieces together. We had to make sure we got the ends connected just right, or when the water was turned back on we'd have problems for sure. That's the way it went, section by section, back and forth, back and forth, until the whole row of pipe had been repositioned so the next rows could be irrigated.

I knew how to clean a house, drive a tractor, hoe weeds and irrigate, but I had no idea what I was supposed to do as a pastor's wife. However, I soon discovered there were plenty of people who could tell me. "The pastor's wife is always the Women's Missionary Union President and has charge of the women's meetings at the church," the ladies of the church explained. "She is also an associational WMU officer and teaches a Sunday school class."

I knew the womens' advice was well-meaning, but I wondered if they'd really considered how different my situation was. Their pastors' wives in the past had been much more mature than I felt. I was an inexperienced teenager driving back and forth 100 miles each way with my husband from college 2 or 3 times a week.

My husband and I also had the job of cleaning the church. At least that was one job I knew I could do well. But teaching? What would I do if they asked me to teach an adult Sunday school class?

Not wanting to appear rebellious or create problems, I dutifully complied with whatever was asked of me. But oh how relieved I was when the class I was given turned out to be the children's class. That was about the highest level I felt capable to teach, and the little kids were a real joy to me. As for the more demanding parts of my new job description, I plastered a smile across my face and began working at the staggering tasks just as I'd tackled those rows of irrigation pipe: one cumbersome piece at a time.

As I struggled to shoulder responsibilities far too heavy for me, I felt more and more inferior. Why couldn't I be more like my husband? I'd always loved people, and they liked me, but Don possessed something special. He never met a stranger or had to grope for the right word. People of all ages and personalities seemed drawn to him, and they weren't disappointed by what they found.

When Don was around, I could "hide" behind him like a little girl hanging onto her father's pant leg, peering out from behind him. He was wise without being a know-it-all, and confident without being pushy. Don always seemed to know exactly what to say to calm tense situations and put people at ease. How I envied my husband's people skills and gift of teaching. However, instead of stepping out and developing my own abilities, I'd found it far less threatening to hide behind Don and depend upon his.

Depending on my husband. That's the way I had lived my life. But after everything collapsed around me, God gently showed me that I not only had found my security in being Don's wife—I had found my identity, as well.

Standing amid the ruins of my past, I realized that a whole lot of things would have to be torn down and discarded before my life could be rebuilt. But I was determined not to allow the pain of giving up parts of myself to keep me from becoming the person God had created me to be.

Choosing The Right Foundation

As God began revealing my innermost heart, He led me to the sobering realization that my marriage had been founded on the false security of an emotionally dependent relationship. Don and I had always been so connected in our emotions that if he was down, I was down. If he was up, I was up. My focus and attention were wrapped up in him. Neither of us had been able to distinguish our inner emptiness and hunger from genuine love. He had needed me, and I had needed him. When he began pulling away and having his needs met through others, I felt as if I were dying inside. When Don withdrew, even God seemed far away.

Now, I was building on the rock-solid security of a rich, fulfilling relationship with the Lord. He was teaching me to recognize and appreciate the gifts and strengths He had placed within me. Deep in the core of my being, I knew that to God, I was not just a number in a nameless, faceless sea of humanity. I was a "hand-made original" thoughtfully designed to fulfill His unique purposes for my life. I was worth dying for. That made me special.

I had learned, almost at the cost of my life, that if I chose to rebel against the laws of love by which God's holy kingdom operated and go my own way, I could not win. On the other hand, if I chose to repent and obey, I could not lose. I could alter the consequences of my sin and rebellion by making a new, right choice. I could have His peace, rest and joy regardless of what was going on around me, and my future was safe in His hands.

For the first time, I caught a tiny glimpse of God's big picture. He was doing something far bigger than me. Something that overcame evil with good. Just as Romans 8:28 declares, "...All things work together and are [fitting into a plan] for good to those who love God and are called according to [His] design and purpose" (Amp.). I had chosen to love, obey and trust God. My times were safe and secure in His mighty hand (Ps. 31:15). No one, not even my husband, could abort God's plan for my life.

I liked the way A.W. Tozer put it:

No one can dissuade Him from His purposes; nothing turn Him

aside from His plans. Since He is omniscient, there can be no unforseen circumstances, no accidents. As He is sovereign, there can be no countermanded orders, no breakdown in authority; and as He is omnipotent, there can be no want of power to achieve His chosen ends. God is sufficient unto Himself for all these things.[2]

As I realized that I did not have to strive, control, or manipulate so His purposes could be accomplished, a peace enveloped me. His ways would be best. His help would always be right on time. God Himself would perfect that which concerned me.

Constructing Boundaries

Part of God's perfecting work involved helping me define healthy spiritual, emotional and physical boundaries.

Out in West Texas where I grew up, neighboring farmers didn't depend too much on fences to define their boundaries. Building and maintaining barbed-wire fences on thousands of acres of land simply wasn't practical. Sure, gates and fences were built where they were needed to keep some things in and other things out, but everyone in the area pretty well knew where one person's property ended and another's started. A farmer's border on the south might be a highway and on the northeast, a ditch. However, just in case of a dispute, an official legal description was put down in black and white at the county records' office.

I understood why it was necessary for property to have clearly defined boundaries, but I'd never realized that people needed boundaries, too. My personal boundaries seemed to have been damaged or too vaguely defined, and I lacked a sense of personal identity. I didn't know who I was in relation to other people physically, emotionally or spiritually. In my relationships, I couldn't distinguish where I and my responsibilities ended and the other person and his or her responsibilities began.

Physical Boundaries

Healthy physical boundaries define our personal space and warn

---

[2]A.W. Tozer, *The Knowledge of the Holy* (c 1961, HarperCollins Publishers, 10 East 53rd Street, New York, NY 10022), p. 175.

us when someone is getting too close. When that personal space is violated, we feel fear and anxiety. However, since I had poor physical boundaries I didn't give enough credence to such feelings. I had no warning signals when someone was mistreating me, no "fences" to protect myself from intruders. That allowed others to take advantage of me.

For example, in one of the churches Don pastored when we were younger, an evangelist conducting a revival for us stayed in our home. He was a very good preacher, and in every service people were giving their hearts to the Lord. Because Don usually stayed late after the services to talk with people, I'd go home early so I could put Tamra to bed.

On the third night of the revival, the evangelist came home about the same time I did, hurried straight to his room and put on his bathrobe. I was busy preparing a snack that the three of us could enjoy when Don came home, so I didn't give his actions a second thought. In a few minutes, he strolled into the kitchen, started chatting, then casually unfastened his robe. He wasn't wearing any clothes underneath!

Pretending I hadn't noticed, I whirled around and walked away, busying myself with making tea and setting the table. At first, I felt more shocked and shamed by what the man had done than if he had cursed me and spat in my face. Then I found myself searching for excuses to explain his behavior. Maybe he hadn't realized what he was doing.... Maybe his thoughts had been somewhere else, and he'd forgotten for a moment that he wasn't at home in his own kitchen with his own wife.... I certainly didn't want to embarrass the man. Surely a minister of the Gospel wouldn't do such a thing on purpose.... Would he? Why, the guy was married and had several kids!

Telling myself that I'd probably become all upset over nothing, I didn't mention the incident to Don when he came home.

The next night I had just put Tamra to bed and was talking on the phone with a church member when the guy walked into the room and did a repeat performance! I spun around with my back to him, praying he would take the hint and go back to his room. Instead, I felt him brush against me. Then he put his hand on my leg. I jerked away. He moved even closer, trying to touch me, caress me. I broke away from his grasp.

"Sorry, I...I've got to go now," I stammered to the startled woman on the other end and slammed down the receiver. Bolting into my bedroom, I shut the door and stood there shaking, begging God to make

Don come home. I felt like a fly caught in a spider web. I was so humiliated, so totally repulsed, so terrified, I thought my heart would hammer out of my chest.

I wrestled over what I should do. Hadn't several more people given their hearts to the Lord in that very evening's service? Think how it would hurt the church if they knew what the evangelist had tried to do. What if by exposing the man's actions I hurt the cause of Christ? That wouldn't be right would it? Besides, if the guy made a habit of behaving like this in the other places where he preached, why was God honoring his ministry? Why were people being saved when he preached?

After a few of the longest minutes in my life, I heard the front door open and Don walked in. Again, for some unexplainable reason, I could neither bring myself to rebuke the man nor tell Don what he was doing.

The rest of the week was a nightmare. I was afraid to be in the same room with the evangelist, even when my husband was in the house. By staying at the church until Don was ready to leave I managed to avoid any more close encounters.

When the week finally ended and the evangelist left, I quietly collapsed in tears of relief. I felt so cowardly. So confused. So stupid and naive. I felt as if I had scrambled eggs for brains. Why? Why hadn't I been able to confront him? Why hadn't I alerted Don to what was happening? On the other hand, if I told, raising questions about the preacher's character, what would happen to the faith and trust of the people in our church—especially the new Christians who had been saved under the man's preaching? Would such a shocking revelation irreparably damage the evangelist's ministry? Imagine how it would hurt his wife and children.... I decided to keep quiet and just forget it. But I've never forgotten the sickening shame, the heart-pounding anxiety triggered inside me by the man's disgusting behavior. Nor have I forgotten the sharp stab of regret I felt a few years later when I learned that the man had died of a heart attack. I couldn't help wondering if things might have turned out differently for the evangelist if I had possessed the courage to confront him, told Don what had happened and the man had been forced to face his sin.

I realize now that my frantic feelings were trying to warn me that the man was consciously, deliberately overstepping my personal boundaries—as well as the bounds of common decency—and he needed to be sharply confronted.

Emotional Boundaries

Unfortunately, my emotional boundaries were not in any better shape. That presented a serious problem, because emotional boundaries serve three important functions. They determine how we feel about ourselves and others. They help shield us from abuse and insults and they enable us to limit the amount of negative feedback and criticism we give ourselves.

My fear of displeasing others and being rejected or forsaken kept me from establishing my own sense of identity. I allowed other people to determine how I felt about myself. I did what others wanted, not what I wanted. My needs and desires didn't matter. They weren't important.

People sometimes asked, "Helen, what do you enjoy doing?" I didn't have a clue. All I'd ever done was what someone else thought I should do. Pleasing, helping and taking care of other people gave me my sense of worth. Consequently, I often spent more of my time and energy inside the boundaries of others, trying to please them, than I did in taking care of my own needs and responsibilities.

"Helen, you're so dependable. I don't know what we would do without you. Do you think you might be able to...?" I was already saying yes before the person finished asking the question. It didn't matter that I already had a list of what seemed like 17,000 things to do. I'd push my own responsibilities aside in order to please someone else.

Many times my helping others just added to their irresponsibility, as well as my own. For example, very early one morning we received a call from a woman who had recently begun attending church. She told us that she was a stripper in a club and that her husband had become very angry when she worked late and arrived home later than usual. They had gotten into a terrible fight, and he had threatened to kill her.

Don and I responded to her plea to come over immediately. Just as we arrived, the woman and her husband left. Their two small children were sitting without any clothes on under the table, eating cereal off the dirty floor. Broken glass from the lamps and other items they had thrown at each other were everywhere. I worked hard the rest of the day sweeping up glass, tending to the children, mopping floors, washing stacks of dirty dishes and doing piles of laundry.

The couple finally came waltzing in the front door late that afternoon, casually blaming their behavior the night before on the fact that they'd had too much to drink. Both of them looked rested, refreshed and ready for another night of chaos. I stared at them in disbelief. Here I was, totally exhausted. Sure, I was glad I'd been able to help their poor little kids, but I realized that all my hard work probably hadn't made one particle of difference. In another day or two the whole place would be in just as bad a shape, or worse.

Free-loaders and pushy people seemed to be attracted to me like a magnet to steel. Sometimes I felt like a pint-sized Statue of Liberty, holding up a sign that read: "Give me your tired, your poor, your huddled masses...." The things I managed to get myself into! Some of it was right, but much of the time I confused compliance for compassion. I simply couldn't say no. I didn't want to offend anyone or have them think badly of me. Besides, coming to another's rescue gave me a feeling of significance.

Spiritual Boundaries

My spiritual boundaries, which were supposed to give me a feeling of value and purpose and define my relationship with God, were poorly defined, too. This deficiency was throwing my life out of balance, for spiritual boundaries, which are based on God's love and purpose for us, promote love for others and positive self-worth.

Our spiritual boundaries can be distorted. They can be manipulated by people or demonic forces seeking to use or control us. They can be damaged when God is portrayed to us as hard and demanding, cold and uncaring, untrustworthy, etc.

Ezekiel 13:22 reveals the overpowering effect that such lies about God's character and personality can have upon God's people: "...With lies you have made the righteous sad and disheartened, whom I have not made sad or disheartened..."(Amp).

That's what had happened to me. I had lost hope and became angry at God because I believed the lies Satan told me about Him....

"You can't trust God. Remember how you gave your family to God, and one week later He snatched your 15-month-old son away from you?" "For years and years you've wept and prayed and begged God to change your husband. Has it done any good? Of course not! You're wasting your breath. He's getting worse, not better. Stop waiting for God to do something. Don't you get it? God is not interested in your petty little problems. He doesn't care. Stop this whining you call `prayer' and take matters into your own hands!"

Learning To Set Limits

I lacked identity and self-worth. I was emotionally dependent upon my husband, and I was a people pleaser. When God first began dealing with me in those areas of need, I had not even known that such a thing as "personal boundaries" existed. Wonderful resources such as Cloud and Townsend's book, Boundaries, that would help guide me later in my journey had not yet been written.[3] But I had asked God to teach me, and He knew what I needed. As I pored over His Word and sought to obey it, the Holy Spirit led me into truth. My vague physical, emotional and spiritual boundaries were gradually defined and reinforced.

Instead of suppressing, ignoring or discounting my feelings, I began learning to acknowledge and listen to them. I did not focus on feelings or allow them to control me. Instead, I tried to identify my feelings and discern the message they were sending. I looked to God's Spirit within my spirit for wisdom and understanding.

As I meditated upon the character and nature of God as revealed in Scripture, I saw an all-powerful, trustworthy God who is just in all His ways and kind in all His doings. I became convinced of God's absolute trustworthiness, His unconditional love and His purposes for my life. I saw that I did not lose my worth or forfeit His best when I made a mistake. I realized that my value does not come from the approval of others, but from a God who will never abandon me or stop loving me. Secure in that assurance, I was able to say no whenever I knew that no was the best answer for me and for the other person. I began responding to needs out of inner compassion instead of outward compliance.

---

[3]Dr. Henry Cloud and Dr. John Townsend, Boundaries (Zondervan Publishing House, Grand Rapids, Michigan 49503, c 1992).

In the past, my own needs had been way down on the list of my priorities. I paid so little attention to them, I couldn't define them for myself, much less communicate my needs to Don or to others. But as time went on, I became more in touch with myself. I defined my likes, dislikes and desires. I learned to recognize the places where my responsibilities stopped. I determined what I could and could not do and defined what was right for me and what was wrong.

As I recognized what my needs and limits were, I began learning to state them clearly so that others were aware of my God-given boundaries. Putting my needs into words and clearly defining my boundaries helped me take responsibility for my own actions. It enabled me to gain self-respect and helped me understand and safeguard my identity. Although I did not use my newly established boundaries to try to manipulate others, I let them know that my boundaries were important and I was serious about them.

Freeing, fulfilling changes were not long in coming. I stopped trying to rescue Don from the consequences of his actions or make excuses for him. I tried to make our home a happy place. Rather than sitting in an empty house and feeling lonely when Don had chosen to be elsewhere, I learned to use those hours to do things I'd been needing or wanting to do. I signed up for classes at the local junior college. I also began ground school, thinking I might enjoy learning to fly a plane.

In the past, I'd been afraid to let Don out of my sight lest he succumb to temptation. Now I had realized that I could not be my husband's "warden." If he made up his mind to be with someone, he was clever enough to arrange it whether or not I was in town. Once I came to that realization, I could pray diligently for Don, I could be there for him when I needed to be, but I stopped trying to play God in his life.

When it became apparent that Don had lied to me about something, I made an effort not to assume the roles of mother or detective. Instead, I'd say something such as, "I need to tell you that I know when you don't tell me the truth." I also stopped trying to be his conscience. As I heard one speaker say, "Instead of talking more to my husband about God, I began talking more to God about my husband."

Get The Root!

Establishing boundaries and forming new behavior patterns wasn't easy. I continued to make more than my share of mistakes. Sometimes I blew it altogether. But I had no intention of giving up. All my years of hoeing weeds and Johnson grass in those endless rows of cotton had taught me patience and persistence.

"You're just makin' more work for yourself later," my dad would say if he caught me becoming slothful with my hoe. "How many times do I have to tell you that if you just chop off Johnson grass level with the ground, instead of diggin' out the roots, it'll grow right back? Now you use that hoe like I showed you, diggin' and diggin', until you've destroyed every last root!"

Knowing he was right and that I'd be in trouble if I didn't listen, I'd get down to business. It took patience and a lot of work up front, but I knew if I could get all the roots the first time I wouldn't have to come back and redo the job.

Now I was just as determined to keep digging away until I'd dug up every last sprig and root of my destructive thought and behavior patterns. If I did a thorough job of it, they wouldn't pop back up to plague me later.

Proof Of His Love

"Those whom the Lord loves He disciplines," writes the author of Hebrews, "and He scourges every son whom He receives.... All discipline for the moment seems not to be joyful, but sorrowful; yet to those who have been trained by it, afterwards it yields the peaceful fruit of righteousness" (Heb. 12:6, 11, NAS). As one looking at those statements from an "afterwards" point of view, I can add my amen.

I never dreamed it could happen. But about mid-point in that seven-year crash course in the School of the Spirit, I actually found myself weeping with gratitude. I heard myself saying, "God, thank You for loving me enough not to answer all those prayers I prayed asking You to change my husband so I wouldn't have to be miserable. Thank You for delivering me through my affliction and for opening my ears to Your voice by adversity."

Now I understood: I had been praying amiss. If God had answered my plea, I might have walked the rest of my life in deception, believing that my husband, not I, was to blame for my inner turmoil. I might never have discovered that my unhappiness and lack of fulfillment were directly attributable to me. My own faulty foundation and misdirected focus on people and circumstances. My unrighteous choices and wrong reactions. My lack of identity and healthy boundaries.

Thank God that He had loved me so much He had refused to allow me to live my whole life thinking I had to be controlled by what was happening around me. If God had changed my husband when I was begging Him to, I might have experienced a counterfeit peace for a time, but it would have evaporated as soon as the next fiery trial came my way. Sooner or later I would have found something or someone else to blame for my emptiness and discontentment.

That's why I could joyfully thank the Lord for not giving in to my tearful pleas. For refusing to back down to my angry threats. For His severe mercy that allowed me to experience suffering in order that I might be healed. For humiliation, that I might learn to walk humbly with my God.

The Little Acorn That God Forgot

It seemed that a lot of my victories were being won behind the scenes in the ordinary, business-as-usual routines of daily life. Letting Don make his own excuses when he missed our son's soccer game or couldn't be located at a meeting he had told me he was attending. Saying no when I was asked to do something that wasn't in my heart to do. Using grouchy old Mrs. Bear to teach myself to respect and appreciate the gifts and unique abilities God had given me.

"All Wrong Mrs. Bear" wasn't the only children's story that helped me learn some important truths during those difficult times. In that same little book was another story that also had become one of my favorites: "The Little Acorn that God Forgot."If I paraphrase it for you, I think you'll understand why.

Once upon a time there was a very small acorn who lived at the top of a tall oak tree. He liked to talk to the clouds as they sailed through the sky. He liked to look up into the blue sky and way, way down at the little squirrels playing on the ground. And he liked to think about God who had made it all.

"God knows all about me," mused Little Acorn. "He put me here in this tree. He knows just where I am and what I like. I'm so glad that God cares about me."

One day the clouds were dark, and the wind was blowing them so fast that it made the big oak tree bend sideways. "Where are you going in such a hurry, clouds?" called Little Acorn.

"We are going to make a storm because the earth needs lots of rain today," called the clouds. "There will be thunder and lightning too, but don't you worry, Little Acorn. God is sending the storm, and He knows all about you. He'll take care of you."

The wind and rain grew stronger. I'm glad God knows where I am and that He takes care of me, thought Little Acorn.

Then he felt a strange thing happen. His little cap that held onto the branch broke loose. Down he fell, landing with a plop in the mud. God must have forgotten about me, he thought sadly. Now what will happen?

At last the sun came out. Little Acorn lay on the ground feeling very sorry for himself. Then he felt himself being lifted up into the air by a squirrel who was busily putting away food for the winter. The squirrel buried him in the ground, then forgot all about him.

Little Acorn was very sad. First God had let him fall from the tree, and now he was buried in the ground where he couldn't see any of the things he had loved. Little Acorn cried and cried. He was sure that God had forgotten all about him. Finally, he cried himself to sleep.

Little Acorn slept all summer and all through the fall and winter. Then, in the spring, he woke up. He felt so different! Why, he wanted to stretch, and STRETCH and STRETCH ! He stretched until he felt like he would break in two; and suddenly, one little arm stretched right out of the ground! Surprised, Little Acorn wiggled the arm around in the air and felt the warm spring sunshine. He kept on stretching and growing, and the arm became bigger and grew branches and leaves. Little Acorn had turned into an oak tree, just like the one he had grown on so long ago.

What a surprise to Little Acorn! Why, God hadn't forgotten him at all. But God had something very good planned that Little Acorn didn't know about.

The oak tree grew and grew until it was large enough to grow other little acorns. It stretched its branches up into the sky and waved at the clouds. When the clouds brought rain, the oak tree covered the little acorns with his leaves and told them, "Don't be afraid. God will take care of you. And even if you think He has forgotten you, He really hasn't. He always knows just where you are and what is best for you."[4]

Development Before Deliverance

Tragedy.... Terror.... Trauma.... Like Little Acorn, I thought God had forgotten me. But now I was managing to break out of the past, and I was stretching in every direction. Finding a new identity in Christ. Building on a solid-rock foundation. Learning and establishing firm, healthy boundaries. Ever so slowly, I was actually beginning to enjoy some of this process called growth!

---

[4]Runyon, All Wrong Mrs. Bear, exerpted from pp. 19-25.

Chapter 5

CHOOSING MY OWN JUDGMENT

"On Christ the Solid Rock I stand. All other ground is sinking sand...." Singing about standing on the rock instead of the sand sounds so simple. But I soon discovered that I was like the person James talks about who is double-minded, unstable in all his ways and like the surf of the sea driven and tossed by the wind (James 1:6,8). It took me three long, hard years of struggling just to get to the point where I was actually beginning to stay on the rock long enough to enjoy it and recognize that it was where I wanted to spend the rest of my life.

I don't think I could over-emphasize how hard those times were. Sometimes I wondered if I would ever smile again, and laughter seemed to belong to another realm and time. Sometimes when the circumstances improved a little, I'd experience a sense of peace and rest and assume I was on the rock. But the Lord has a very effective way of letting us know whether the peace and rest we are experiencing are genuine or counterfeit: He allows things to change for the worse. When that happens, if our peace is from God, we will experience some emotion and feeling, but we will still have peace in our spirit.

On the other hand, if the peace we're feeling is just an emotional response to circumstances changing for the better, when they change for the worse our pseudo peace and rest will vanish. Then we will realize we were living at the edge of the sand instead of on the rock.

As time went by, my heart became more established on the rock. That certainly does not mean I've never again found myself in the sand. Not at all! Living on the rock is a daily choice. It can be a many-times-a-day choice. Satan is so subtle, our flesh so persistent. But once we have become established on the rock and we're experiencing God's peace, rest and joy, alarms start going off when we find ourselves battling inner turmoil. We review the circumstance and realize that our focus has shifted to people and problems instead of God and His promises. At that moment we have a choice. We can indulge in those negative emotions and have a pity party in the sand, or we can refocus on the Lord and get back onto the rock.

Learning to live and build on the rock is a lot like learning to walk. We stand, and we fall. We stand, and we fall. But I had rather fall, get back up and keep trying than crawl the rest of my life for fear I might stumble.

My Self-Chosen Judgement

As God performed His purifying work in my life, having to face my hurtful ways and secret sins was sometimes overwhelming. One of the most difficult things to see was my proud, judgmental heart.

I had never realized that I'd spent most of my life judging people. Somewhere early in my youthful journey, I'd picked up the idea that being spiritual was measured by what you didn't do. If you didn't smoke, drink, play cards, go the horse races, commit adultery, or go to movies on Sunday then you were spiritual. Never mind the fact that you judged or gossiped about everyone who did those "awful" things.

I was familiar with Christ's warning, "Do not judge lest you be judged. For in the way you judge, you will be judged" (Matt. 7:1,2 NAS). I'd read Job 36:17: "...If you are filled with the judgment of the wicked, judgment and justice will keep hold on you" (Amp.). But somehow, I'd never taken those spiritual laws seriously.

I'd never had trouble accepting the reality of God's physical laws. Knowing I'd find the sun coming up in the east every morning gave me security. I respected the law of gravity, the laws governing electricity, the laws of nutrition, the laws of health, etc. I had seen them operate. I had observed their effects.

For example, when I was a child, one of my schoolmates hurried home one afternoon to get ready for her birthday party. Thinking the red liquid in a jar on the kitchen counter was Kool-Aid, she drank anti-freeze. Her horrified parents rushed her to the hospital as soon as they discovered her mistake, but it was too late. The poisonous anti-freeze, once ingested, damaged her brain and major organs. My schoolmate died, even though she sincerely thought she was drinking Kool-Aid.

God's spiritual laws, like His physical laws, are absolute, and they will operate. Whether we know them or not. Whether we like them or not. Whether we believe them or not. Law is law.

Like many Christians, I'd read scriptures about the law of judging, but I'd read with a "ho-hum, it-couldn't-really-be-that-important" attitude. Consequently, because I hadn't taken God's command seriously I had judged harshly, and I had judged often. I had judged others for the very things of which I myself was capable. I hadn't known it at the time, but I was choosing my own judgment.

I did not realize that whenever we judge, consciously or not, a law is set in motion. Eventually, the seed of judgment we have sown produces fruit. That fruit may be anger, for example. We become angry and say things we shouldn't. Then we repent: "God, I'm sorry for getting mad and losing my temper. Please help me never do that again." But before long something else happens, and we throw another tantrum. "Oh, no, God!" we cry. "Where are You? Why aren't You answering my prayers and changing me?" The simple truth is that we're not being changed because we're confessing the fruit, not the root.

Bitter fruit comes from a bitter root. It is the root—the harsh judgment we made regarding someone else—that is producing the fruit: "I'll never be like my mother." "When I grow up, I'll never act like my father." "Can you believe that person calls himself a Christian and does such a thing? Why, I'd never ever think of doing that!"

When we judge, the process is set in motion. Unless that bitter root judgment is cut off through repentance, in the way we judged we will be judged.

As a girl, I'd judged wives who vented their pain and fury on a drunken or adulterous husband who came sneaking through the door long after midnight. And I had made myself two promises. I will never marry a man who would do such things. Furthermore, when I'm married, I'll never be the kind of wife who becomes so filled with self-pity that she turns into a depressed, angry person.

Remembering those earnest promises, I'd breathed a contented sigh after marrying a preacher. Thank goodness, I'd never have to worry about my marriage. But years later, after blowing up in Don's face as he stepped through the doorway offering his usual "I was preparing for

Sunday's sermon and had to stay late and do a little counseling" excuse, my pious little promises came back to haunt me. "...For in the way you judge, you will be judged."

I had felt very justified in condemning my husband and his unfaithfulness to me. I had judged him severely. I couldn't imagine a Christian—much less, a pastor—being that sinful. "Judge not, lest ye be judged...."

Furthermore, I'd judged God Himself, believing He was unjust and unconcerned. After all, I saw a much greater anointing upon my husband than I had ever experienced. How could an all-seeing, holy God be so blind, so unfair?

And oh, how I'd judged spiritual leaders and other believers who fell into sin. I simply couldn't comprehend how men and women who called themselves Christians could stoop to such levels and hurt the cause of Christ.

So what happened next? God allowed me to see that "he that judges is guilty in his heart of the same things" (Rom. 2:1-3). I deliberately chose to do a thing so detestable it made the plots of a lot of soap operas pale in comparion. "For in the way you judge, you will be judged....."

I had never grasped what the Scriptures meant by declaring that God's ways are not our ways, His thoughts are not our thoughts and His timing is not our timing. I had never comprehended that His merciful gaze could penetrate the filthy cloak of the sinner and read the yearnings and thoughts and intents of the broken heart beating inside.

A shaft of shame pierced my soul when I realized that Don's heart had never been like mine. He didn't judge others by what his eyes saw, or make decisions about others based upon what his ears heard. His assessments of people and their situations had always seemed so fair and compassionate and righteous, compared with mine. I'd seen him broken with sorrow for his own sin and for the sins and failures of others.

The awful truth blasted me broadside: I had a stern, condemning, self-righteous heart of judgment that hated sin in others but couldn't see it in myself. Don had a tender, teachable, repentant heart that mourned over its failures, pled for deliverance and hungered after righteousness. That's why there could be an anointing on his ministry. That's why God could bless.

"Judge not, lest ye be judged...." How many people had I judged and condemned unmercifully? With a sickening feeling in the pit of my stomach, I thought again of how many times through the years I had judged and condemned women who'd had abortions—until I was faced with the choice myself.

I'd always believed in the sanctity of life. I'd never been able to consider the three month-old fetus I'd held in my hand after I miscarried to be anything other than my precious little baby. I had asked God to show me the sex of the baby and had even given her a name. The act of deliberately taking the life of a tiny, defenseless baby inside its mother's womb was absolutely unthinkable to me, and I condemned any woman who did. Then, I went through a situation that gave me an understanding and compassion for other women who've faced that decision.

I can still remember the sick, panicky feeling deep inside when I was involved in the affair and, for a few days, thought I was pregnant. Don would have known it was impossible for the baby to be his, and I would always have known for sure that it couldn't be. Besides, having another person's baby would destroy my already damaged family and create such a magnitude of problems, I couldn't even fathom having the grace to survive. Satan added to the turmoil in my mind by mockingly invading my imaginations with pictures of a baby who looked just like the person I was involved with.

For days I felt as if I were locked inside a torture chamber with a vice pulling apart my body, soul and spirit. I knew the mental torture I was experiencing was due to a decision forming in my mind that was a direct, extreme violation of what I believed in my spirit: the decision that I would have no choice but to have an abortion. For the first time in my life I knew what it was to feel deep compassion for women who had aborted babies.

Much to my relief, about a week later it was confirmed that I was not pregnant. Whether or not I would actually have been able to have an abortion, I will never know. But I do know that God made me vividly aware of this one thing: "Therefore you are without excuse, every man of you who passes judgment, for in that you judge another, you condemn yourself; for you who judge practice the same things" (Rom. 2:1, NAS).

From that point on, I continued to oppose abortion, but I could no longer judge those who had one. Instead, I prayed compassionately for them, asking God to forgive them and minister to them.

But what about all those other times I'd self-righteously set myself up as someone else's judge when I didn't know his or her heart and hadn't experienced his or her pain and struggles? By judging others, how many seeds of bitter judgment had I sown in the garden of my own heart? How many of those seeds were springing to life and beginning to sprout even at that moment?

The very thought filled my heart with holy fear. Why? Because I had grown up around soil and seeds, sowing and reaping, and I knew that one tiny seed, when planted, produces more seeds. I was overcome with conviction. Oh, Lord! What had I done? If I did not receive God's mercy what would become of my life? Falling on my face, I begged God to forgive me and help me obliterate the bitter root judgments in my heart.

Dealing With Bitter Root Judgements

I've learned more about roots of bitterness since that time years ago. I now know that bitter root judgments are one of the most common, most basic sins in human relationships—especially marital relationships. We almost always marry someone who has a bitter root judgment that is attracted like a magnet to ours, and vice versa.

As I shared before, I had made a bitter root judgment of women who angrily met their husbands at the door when they came in late at night under suspicious circumstances. However, it was not the harsh judgment I had made and never dealt with that caused Don's behavior. Don also had a bitter root judgment which he had never addressed. It was a judgment he had made against his father for never approving of even one friend he brought home.

Whenever Don came in late and said to me, "I've been at the church office, studying and ministering to so and so," I immediately feared the worst. Wanting to warn and protect my husband I sometimes promptly pointed out the 2% that I felt in my spirit was wrong with the person he'd been ministering to rather than pointing out the 98% that was right. When I did, Don would react to me with such intense anger that it simply didn't make sense. What neither of us realized was that my anger stemmed from the bitter root judgment I'd made as a young girl, and the anger Don vented upon me in return was really toward his dad.

Bitter root judgments can wreak havoc in a marriage—especially if you're the stubborn type that says, "I may be wrong, but the person I'm married to is worse," or "Why can't my spouse change first? Why do I always have to make the first move?" That attitude can't get to the cross.

The fact that I'm having a problem in my marriage doesn't mean my marriage is not working. It can be a sign that it is working! You see, nothing is more devastating to selfishness than being married. Marriage is a way to work Christ's character in us. If we have a bitter root judgment in our life, Jesus loves us so much and so desires that we become conformed to His image that He will keep allowing circumstances to come until we finally choose to deal with that root.

Accepting with Joy

I'm learning more and more that it's one thing to pray, "Oh, God, let Your power change my circumstances; it's another to pray, "Oh, God, let Your love change me." I've heard sermons about the eternal reign of Christ some day, and they've been good. But for now, I know I need to be concerned with His internal reign in me in this life. How do I go about allowing Christ to set up His internal rule in my heart and letting His love change me?

As strange as it may sound, I can begin the process of obliterating a bitter root of judgment by choosing to accept with joy that particular circumstance over which I had no control but which God allowed. I'm not talking about blissfully denying a problem, suppressing my emotions, or docilely allowing others to run over me. Neither do I mean that I cannot take part in helping and delivering others in their difficult or oppressive circumstances. Nor should I passively submit to sin, evil or temptation. I should not just sigh, "Oh, well. God let this happen, so I'm supposed to submit to it." No. I have to hear God and be obedient to Him.

Accepting with joy all that God permits to happen to me means not being resentful or reacting with bitterness and unforgiveness. Accepting with joy eliminates self-pity, complaining, murmuring and unforgiveness.

Oswald Chambers said, "Suffering is the heritage of the bad, the penitent and of the Son of God. Each one ends at the cross. The bad thief was crucified, the penitent thief was crucified, and the Son of God was crucified." God did not insulate His own Son from the effects of the evil choices of others. Yet Jesus accepted all that His Father permitted to happen to Him. He did not become angry, bitter or resentful. His attitude was, "I delight to do Thy will, O my God."

There were no "second causes" in the life of Joseph, who was sold as a slave by his brothers, and there are no "second causes" in my life, either. It's not what happens to me that counts. It's my reaction to what happens to me that is important. I am to react in love.

Some people say, "But I can't do that. I don't want to be a hypocrite. I don't feel loving. I feel hurt and furious. I feel I'm at a breaking point." However, a simple illustration from everyday life shows the fallacy of such thinking. When our daughter was a baby she didn't sleep well. While babies were supposed to be quietly sleeping, Tamra often was restless or screaming. Some nights I was exhausted and didn't feel like getting out of bed and tending to my baby daughter, but I did it anyway. Did that make me a hypocrite? Of course not. Neither am I a hypocrite if I choose to walk as I really am in Christ instead of reacting according to my feelings at the moment.

I have been placed in this world and allowed this human experience over which I seemingly have no control. Why? That I might meet and overcome evil with good. (See Rom. 12:21). That I might overcome difficulty, sin and sorrow. Obviously, the only right attitude of heart is the one Jesus had—accepting and delighting to do God's will.

Renewing My Mind

Renewing my mind by hiding God's Word in my heart is a necessary step to accepting with joy what God permits. The more I allow the Lord to control my mind, the more my inner reaction to difficulties will be peace and joy.

How does God's Word say I am to react to pressures and problems?

"Rejoice always, pray without ceasing, in everything give thanks; for this is the will of God in Christ Jesus for you" (1 Thess. 5:16-18).

"My brethren, count it all joy when you fall into various trials, knowing that the testing of your faith produces patience. But let patience have its perfect work, that you may be perfect and complete, lacking nothing" (James 1:2-4). "...We also exult in our tribulations, knowing that tribulation brings about perseverance; and perseverance, proven character; and proven character, hope; and hope does not disappoint..." (Rom. 5:3, NAS).

"Blessed are you when men cast insults at you, and persecute you, and say all kinds of evil against you falsely, on account of Me. Rejoice, and be glad, for your reward in heaven is great" (Matt. 5:11, 12, NAS).

"...We know that all things work together for good to those who love God, to those who are the called according to His purpose" (Rom. 8:28).

On the other hand, if I refuse to obey God's Word and do not joyfully accept those things permitted by God over which I have no control, I will find myself in a prison of resentment and self-pity. My lack of joyful acceptance will have a destructive influence on my personality, character and physical health.

God's command about "joyfully accepting" definitely let me know that my natural, human ways aren't His ways and my natural, human thoughts are not His thoughts. Yet,it is in times of testing through pain, sorrow and affliction that I discover what God can do. God allows no circumstance to come into my life that cannot be transformed into ultimate blessing. The greater the evil, the greater the opportunity to fashion out of it everlasting good. No evil done to me can ultimately destroy God's purpose for my life because those evil actions and their effects will be compensated for by God Himself.

Freely Forgiving

Though I chose to forgive the offender and the offense out of which my bitter root judgment grew, in myself I could not forgive the past and bury it at the Cross of Christ. I could do it alone: It is Christ within me. Trusting Him to do in me what I cannot do for myself, I choose to forgive. I release the past and let it go. I stop dwelling on and talking about the offense, making myself look good and the offender look bad.

Praying for the Offender

It is impossible to remain bitter toward a person for whom I am faithfully, sincerely praying. I am not to use prayer as an occasion to rehearse the person's faults and shortcomings. Instead of speaking more harsh, merciless words of judgment, I can begin speaking words of blessing over those who have wounded or wronged me.

Choosing to Walk By Faith, Not Sight

Whenever I feel that old emotion from my bitter root judgment rising within, I choose to walk by faith (trusting and obeying God's Word) rather than sight (emotion). Once the bitter root judgment is recognized and dealt with, the law of judgment that says the same judgment I meted out to others will be measured again to me becomes powerless and has no effect in that area.

At first, choosing to trust and obey God's Word rather than giving in to my emotions may be very hard to do. For example, my friend wrestled with this truth after she was raped by three men who broke into her home. The men tied up her husband, then raped her in the bedroom where her children were sleeping. In addition to her pain and shame, my friend was terrified that her children would wake up and be killed by the savage, angry men. She was also certain that one of the men had AIDS. Though the case was investigated thoroughly, her attackers were never apprehended.

In spite of all the counseling my friend received after that traumatic event, she couldn't get rid of an ever-present blockage to her emotional healing. Then she allowed God to show her the hearts of the men who had forever altered her life and prayed that God would forgive them. Realizing that, in the spiritual realm, the men really had not known what they were doing, (see Lu. 23:34.), she voiced her forgiveness and prayed that God would send someone into their lives who would share with them His love and forgiveness. She left them in the hands of a loving God who is concerned with all mankind. As she prayed, her petitions were so above natural human thoughts and ways, I knew she was in touch with God's own thoughts and ways. My heart was flooded with a certainty that while she was praying for the men who had attacked her so mercilessly, something supernatural happened that would allow good to overcome evil. The freedom she felt was so overwhelming, she asked me to use her story, hoping other victims could be released from their prison within.

Reaping A Different Harvest

From the moment I recognized the truth about the law of judging and saw my proud, judgmental heart, whenever the Holy Spirit reminded me of someone or something I had judged in the past, I could not wait to ask God for forgiveness. I attacked the critical, insensitive words I had spoken with the same unyielding perseverance my dad had taught me to use against the despised Johnson grass craving to claim his farm land.

Once I had been like the proud Pharisee whom Jesus referred to in the parable He addressed "to certain ones who trusted in themselves that they were righteous, and viewed others with contempt" (Luke 18:9, NAS). Once I'd prayed, "God, I thank Thee that I am not like other people: swindlers, unjust, adulterers, or even like this tax-gatherer." Now, I stood in the humble sandals of the tax-gatherer, unwilling to lift up my eyes to heaven, beating my breast, saying, "God be merciful to me, the sinner!"

I had sown to the wind and I'd reaped the whirlwind. Like rootless, fruitless, worthless chaff, my life had been blown away. Now I was determined to begin sowing to the Spirit that I might reap a harvest of righteousness.

Chapter 6

LEARNING TO HEAR AND OBEY

My feeble faith had been nourished in Colorado through the "manna verses" God made real to me as the doctor's wife read His Word aloud each day. Once I was well enough to "gather manna" for myself, I had continued reading five Psalms and a chapter from Proverbs every day, plus following my custom of attempting to read the Bible through each year. By reading five Psalms a day, I read through the book of Psalms every month. That's how I had lived those first three years. It was as if a doctor had said, "The Psalms are the medicine you need to take in order to get well."

Each day God gave me a manna verse that answered the question or addressed the problem I was battling that particular moment. Those special scriptures were literally healing to my soul. They put hope and life back into me. They taught me how to thrive in my walk with God—not just survive.

I found myself reading the Bible from a different perspective. Characters who had once been the heroes of the nice little Bible stories I'd told my children became real, flesh- and-blood human beings whose lives exemplified the truths that God was endeavoring to teach me. For example, as I meditated on the story of Joseph, I saw a young man who could have focused on his feelings and problems and become a bitter victim. Instead, Joseph became a victor by choosing to focus on His God and the promises He had given him years before. I knew the same choice is always available to me, regardless of my situation.

Turning Tests Into Teachable Moments

I could imagine Joseph saying, "Here I am in this Egyptian dungeon, God. What do You want me to do? What do You want me to say? What do You want to teach me? My life is in Your hands. Show me how to help the keeper of this prison manage more expertly and efficiently and improve the conditions for us all. Shine through me and transform the very atmosphere of this dark, evil place. Speak to these hopeless men in dreams and visions of the night; then give me the supernatural wisdom to interpret so they may know there is a God in heaven who loves them. Use my lonely hours to deepen my relationship with You and to help prepare me for the tasks and responsibilities You have planned for me in the future."

Deciding I would be as I envisioned Joseph to be, I made up my mind to turn my times of testing into teachable moments.

Basing Joy Upon Hearing, Obeying and Trusting God

As I studied the experiences of Paul and Silas, I saw men who heard God for themselves, obeyed what they heard, then rested in the knowledge that they were in His hands. At first, when I read in Acts 16 about Paul and Silas praising God in a prison at midnight after being brutally beaten for preaching about Jesus, the diverse factors in their story didn't compute. They'd been divinely called in a vision to preach the Gospel in Macedonia and had obeyed. They were falsely accused and unjustly sentenced. After receiving many blows with rods, they were thrown into the inner prison, their feet fastened in stocks. Yet at midnight, incredulous inmates were listening as Paul and Silas prayed and sang hymns of praise to God!

I couldn't imagine how such a thing could be until I realized that their joy was not based upon circumstances. Paul and Silas could sing because they knew they had heard and obeyed God. Therefore, they could trust Him in the midst of anything they encountered while walking that path of obedience.

I couldn't imagine being able to hear and obey God like Joseph, Paul and Silas, but I wanted to overflow with joy and praise based upon hearing, trusting and obeying God. I hungered to possess such God-glorifying faith. That became the prayer of my heart.

"Being" Versus "Doing"

At first, hearing God was even more difficult than I had imagined. Changing from a law-and-works mentality to a grace mentality—from "doing" versus "being"—was not easy. My first thought had always been, Okay, tell me what to do.

All my life I have worked very hard. I'm a real "doer." If it takes doing 150 things in order to reach a goal, then I'll do them. I will go without sleep. I will go without food. I will go without rest. It goes well with my workaholic mentality.

My life on the sand, living on the side of law and works, had been based upon "doing" in order to "be." Now the order was being reversed. Jesus was saying, "No, there's nothing you can do. I've already done it. Your first responsibility is to be. Be on the rock. Be obedient. Then, when I speak to you, do what I say."

Learning to Hear and Obey God's Voice

I hadn't heard God's voice very often in the past. But maybe He hadn't spoken very specifically because I hadn't asked very specifically. I decided to give that a shot and see if it worked. Wonder of wonders, it did! Using experiences in my own life and instruction from the book, Hearing God, by my good friend, Peter Lord, God taught me several practical steps to hearing His voice.

1. Ask specifically.

When a decision or situation arose about which I really needed to hear from God, I focused on God, not on people or circumstances. I asked Him specific questions, and I asked Him to answer. I became so brave that I even asked God where a belt was that I'd lost and hadn't seen in weeks. About two days later I woke up one morning with the thought that I should look underneath the cushion in a particular chair. I jumped out of bed, raced to the chair and pulled up the cushion. There was my lost belt.

I learned if I want to hear God's voice, I should ask Him specific questions and expect Him to answer.

2. Bind every hindering voice, and open your spiritual ears to His voice.

Aware that every voice that speaks to me is not God's, in the name of Jesus I bound the voice of every spirit except the Holy Spirit. I bound the voice of Satan and his demon powers. I bound the voice of my own human desires and reasoning, for my thoughts are not God's thoughts and my ways are not His ways. Then I asked the Lord to open the ears of my spirit to His voice, sharpening my spiritual sensitivity so I could hear His answer. I asked Him to speak to me, in His own time and in His own way, and tell me if there was something He wanted me to say or do in response to the problem or situation.

Late one night, our telephone rang. I answered and heard the cry of a desperate young woman pleading to come talk with me right then. I was so weary I felt like insisting that she wait until morning, but my spirit said, "Tell her to come right on over."

When she arrived, the young woman apologized for her urgent demands to see me so late at night. A sob caught in her throat as she explained that she had a life or death decision to make before morning and that the turmoil she was experiencing in her heart was unbearable. I learned that in only a few hours she was scheduled to have an abortion at a clinic out of town. Every fiber of my being understood her pain as she wept, confessing that she'd had an affair and was pregnant. "I'm not married, and I already have 2 children," she sobbed. "I simply cannot afford to provide for another one. There's just no way. I'm already stretched financially as far as I can go."

At first, I tried talking to her about the many childless couples longing for a baby and how much my adopted baby had meant to me. Though she listened politely, I sensed that my line of reasoning was getting nowhere. "I...I could never give my baby to anyone else," she explained brokenly. "That's why abortion seems like my only choice."

Realizing that her pain and anguish had confused her thinking to the point that killing her unborn baby seemed more right and merciful than relinquishing it into the loving arms of another, I instantly stopped relying upon my own human reasoning. Silently lifting her need to God,

I opened up the ears of my spirit to hear His voice.

As soon as I asked God to give me the right words to share, He dropped His answer into my heart. Looking the young woman right in the eyes, I said, "If you will have this baby, my husband and I will support it as if it were ours. If you feel unable to care for it physically and emotionally, I will take the baby and care for it and love it as my own until you are able. We will pay for whatever you cannot afford.

I made that promise, very much aware of the sacrifices it would involve. But those seeds of hope were taken somehow from the heart of God and implanted in the troubled heart of that young woman, supplying the freedom and strength she needed to keep her baby. After expressing her gratitude, she hugged me goodbye. As I stood at the door in the chilly night air and watched her hurrying to her car, I felt strangely warmed inside. She was not the only one at peace. I knew, in the realm of the spirit, that the struggle I myself had experienced regarding an abortion had been settled. All was well with my soul.

As God in His sovereign mercy would have it, everything the young mother needed for the baby was provided. One December morning she phoned to tell me how awesomely God had ministered to her needs. She also shared that the small church she attended had asked if her newborn baby could represent Baby Jesus in their live nativity scene. "As the lights glowed over the manger and I looked down at my baby wrapped in warm blankets and sleeping peacefully on the hay, grateful tears ran down my cheeks. I knew I had to call and thank you again."

I nodded, too overcome by emotion to speak. My heart was thanking God for letting me hear His voice and for giving me the grace to walk by faith.

3. Listen expectantly for God's answer.

Deaf to Satan's whisper, open to God's Spirit and broken to my own will, I listened. Sometimes I heard immediately. Sometimes the answer came in a few days. If I didn't hear, I just kept waiting. I remembered the question I had asked Him, and I knew I would recognize His answer when it came. Sometimes God spoke directly to my heart. Sometimes He spoke to me through His Word. At times He spoke to me through a song, or through the words or writings of others. The important thing was that He spoke.

4. Refuse to react to hurts, etc. Choose to hear God, then respond accordingly.

Simple lessons on hearing and obeying God's voice began coming to me in the business of everyday life. He even transformed telephone calls into teachable moments.

My mind was a million miles away when I answered the phone one day, but it beamed back down to earth in a hurry when the woman calling launched into an angry tirade. "I saw you go out of your way to speak to that new woman in church last Sunday while you totally ignored me. You never have time for anyone unless they're wealthy or influential. Obviously, she was both, and I am neither. Well, I just want you to know that I think it's a sin and a shame for a pastor's wife to...."

My mind was reeling. My heart was pounding. I could feel my anger beginning to surface like rising streams of bubbles in a pot just about to boil. It would have felt so good to shout, "That is a lie! Shut up a minute, and I'll tell you a thing or two!" (And that would have been all it took to send us both right over the screaming edge.) But what was I supposed to say? Her rapid-fire accusations were ricocheting off the walls. Both of us could wind up even more wounded if I said the wrong thing.

Calm down, Helen, I reminded myself. This woman is not your problem. She didn't make you angry. She is not taking away your peace. Look where you're standing right now. You've stepped off the rock, and you're up to your knees in sand.

"I'm sorry, Father," I silently repented in my heart. "Please forgive me for taking my eyes off You so quickly and focusing on what she is saying. How should I answer these false accusations? What do You want me to do?

"Tell her that you love her and that you know she has some really deep hurts.."

What? Where on earth had that come from? Surely that wasn't God.

"Tell her."

There it was again. Well, what did I have to lose. She already sounded as if she hated me anyway. I waited.... She'd have to draw a breath sometime, and when she did, I would—

"While you've been talking to me I've been praying about you, and I believe the Lord has told me that you have some really deep hurts. I want you to know that I really love you...."

I heard a surprised gasp. Then a strangled sob. She was crying!

"I'm sorry," the woman managed to say as she continued to weep. "I don't know what got into me. I've just been through so much, and I've needed a friend to talk to.... I've never had anyone who cared about me, who didn't reject me...."

Instantly, the direction of the conversation had shifted! I couldn't believe it. How could one little soft-spoken sentence have....? It was God! God had spoken to me! God had given me just the words that a desperate woman needed to hear! I listened quietly as she shared many unhealed hurts. Later, I was able to introduce her to some ladies in the church who befriended her. From the moment that day when God gave me just the words she so desperately needed to hear, that woman became my friend.

5. Don't assume that you already know what to say or do. Ask for God's specific word for that specific situation.

Two weeks after that first angry caller, I was shocked to receive an irate call from a different woman. That sort of thing had rarely, if ever, happened to me. What was going on, anyway? The woman's words were biting. Vicious. Her accusations regarding a women's meeting she had attended were totally unfounded. How had she scrambled the facts so badly?

Well, no matter. I wasn't angry or upset. I already knew exactly what I was going to say, but I repeated the words in my mind, just to make sure.... "I love you, and I know you have some really deep hurts...." "I love you, and I know you have some really deep...." I listened complacently, waiting for the pause, before she fired off another volley....

"I didn't say that."

The words brought me up short, convicting me sharply and snapping me back to reality. Why, I hadn't been listening to God at all. I hadn't even asked Him what to do. I'd just surveyed the circumstances, thumbed through my mental file of possible responses and come up with the solution that worked so well two weeks before. How careless. How callous!

"I'm sorry, God. Please forgive me," I prayed silently. "You hear what she is saying to me. Tell me what You want me to say or do...."

"Hang up the phone."

What? Yeah, sure, I muttered to myself, assuming the prompting must have come from my own wounded pride. Wouldn't that be lovely? To have your pastor's wife hang up on you! I'd never done that. I just couldn't.

"Hang up the phone."

I blinked in surprise. It was that still, small Voice again. No doubt about it. It was God. And He had just told me to hang up the phone! Who would ever believe that one? The woman was still bombarding me with accusations when I very, very timidly and ever so gently placed the receiver back on the hook. Then I went peacefully on my way, knowing that I hadn't hung up because of what she was saying, or because I didn't want to listen, or for revenge. I was just trying to be obedient to God.

I have no idea how many more clips of ammunition the woman wasted before discovering that she was firing into thin air. But the next Sunday, when I saw her at church, she was subdued and polite as could be. (Come to think of it, she did look at me rather strangely.) Neither of us ever mentioned the incident. We never became close friends, either, but that was okay, too. I knew I had obeyed God and had done exactly what He instructed me to do.

I also knew He'd taught me an important lesson: Just because God told me to respond in a certain way on one occasion and it worked, I should never assume that I can automatically use the same response in a similar situation and get similar results. No. I must hear and obey God's specific word for each particular set of circumstances.

6. Don't automatically assume that God's will for someone else is also God's will for you—or vice versa.

I was sitting in church one Sunday morning, absent-mindedly listening to the usual announcements, when my attention was suddenly arrested: "Our college students will have the opportunity to participate in an upcoming missions trip to Guatemala where we will be ministering to former communist guerrillas in a remote resettlement camp up in the jungle." The date of the trip and a few other details were given, the other announcements were made and the service continued. However, it went on without me. My mind was still focused on that announcement and a strange impression that kept surfacing in my spirit.

You are to go on this missions trip to Guatemala.

No, that can't be right, I argued. Don and I had already agreed to go with our high schoolers on a ski trip to Colorado during that same time. It wasn't that I was crazy about snow skiing. On my first and only skiing adventure I had collided with a tree, knocked my arm out of the socket and had to be taken down the mountain on a little sled. This time, I'd already made plans to warm myself by the fireplace inside the lodge, sip hot chocolate, catch up on my reading and let everybody else face the cold and the trees.

I wasn't that excited about the ski trip, but it never occurred to me that I had any alternative but to follow through on the agreement Don and I had already made. Yet for the rest of that afternoon and evening, the strange impression stayed with me: You are to go on the missions trip to Guatemala.

After church that night, Don and I were talking about the day. Out of the blue, I heard myself saying, "I had the strangest sensation this morning in church that I was to go to Guatemala on that missions trip."

"That's just what the Lord said to me that you were to do, Helen," said Don, nodding in agreement.

"What? Well, why didn't you tell me?"

Don laughed. "Do you think I would have the nerve to tell you that I believed God wanted you to go to some remote resettlement camp in the Guatemalan jungle and wanted me to go skiing in Colorado?"

"You're right," I said, laughing with him. "If I hadn't already heard the same thing from the Lord, that would not have been what I wanted to hear from you."

Well, so much for toasting marshmallows and sipping hot chocolate. What kind of boots and bug repellant would I need? What about my hair dryer? Oh, my!

7. Do the possible thing God tells you to do, and trust Him to take care of the impossibles beyond your reach or resources.

The trip into the Guatemalan jungle was a very interesting

experience, to say the least. No privacy. Washing our food in Clorox water. A hair-do that looked as if it had never even heard of a blow dryer—or shampoo either, for that matter.

When we finally arrived, I found that in some respects the resettlement camp resembled a prison camp. There were guards, and the only people who seemed to be allowed to leave were the men going out into the jungle areas to work. Former Kekchi Indian guerrillas were being retrained before being returned to their villages, but I was surprised to see old people, women and children there, as well. Many had lost their homes or families when their village was attacked, and now they had nowhere to go. Some were orphaned children found wandering in the jungle. Some were mothers and widows.

Things I'd always considered absolute necessities turned out to be luxuries. In a camp of over 300 people, there was not one spoon, fork, knife, plate or cooking utensil. Not one roll of toilet paper. Not one diaper—and there were plenty of babies who could have used one. No kitchen. No tables or chairs. Someone had thoughtfully attempted to make a toilet of sorts for us American women, but curious eyes could peer at us through inch-wide cracks in the makeshift shelter where we dressed and slept.

I watched with wonder and respect as desperately poor, but resourceful, people carried on the business of living. The menu for every meal was always the same: beans and tortillas. Large metal barrels filled with dry beans or corn to be ground into meal had been sent in by the government. The empty barrels became pots in which beans were cooked over open fires. The tops of the barrels, cut out and laid on glowing coals, became griddles upon which the women cooked the tortillas made from the corn they'd ground. Sticks were the cooking utensils used to turn the tortillas and to stir the beans as they cooked. The tortillas then became plates upon which the beans were served.

One night as we were using a little generator to show the Jesus film that had been dubbed into the people's language, a dirty, dark-eyed darling little girl wandered over and sat in my lap. She looked to be about two years old. I cuddled and rocked her, stroking her tangled hair.

The film ended, a simple Gospel message was presented; then the people, many with tears still shining in their eyes, smiled and nodded their appreciation and walked away. Finally, no one was left except soldiers holding machine guns. Still I kept sitting there, waiting for the little girl's mother to come back and get her. Cradling the toddler, I walked over to their leader and told him the girl's mother had forgotten her. His dark face softened as he looked at the child sleeping peacefully in my arms. "No," he replied through an interpreter, "she has no parents. We found her and her little brother wandering around in the jungle two days ago." The soldier turned and pointed into the shadows. "She stays over there with the other children who have no parents. An old man stays with them. All of his family were killed, so he has no one, either."

Shivering in the cool air, I made my way through the shadows. Wrapping my precious bundle in a tattered blanket and a warm, protective cocoon of prayer, I gently laid the child on a board beside the other sleeping children and walked away with tears running down my cheeks. It was one of the hardest things I've ever had to do.

We prayed with a lot of people. Grief-stricken young mothers who sobbed as they told us through an interpreter how their children had been lost in the jungle during the attack in which their husbands or other family members had been killed. Tired, lonely-eyed old people. Weary women. Hopeless, empty-hearted men. And children. Lots and lots of children.

I didn't know their language, so I prayed all the time that the Lord would help me express His love to the little kids. I'm not a singer—I can't even carry a tune—so I was surprised when the Lord told me to sing to the children. After that, I'd go to them one by one wherever I encountered them during the day. Kneeling down, I'd take hold of the child's hands, look into its eyes and sing, "Jesus made you special. You're the only one of your kind. God has given you a body and a bright, healthy mind. He has a special purpose that He wants you to find...."

I can't even remember all the words now, or even who wrote them, but I must have sung the song 500 times that week. Some of the children stretched out their hands when they saw me coming, wanting me to sing it to them again. I sang the song gladly, knowing that if God had told me to sing it, He would honor its message of love and hope and speak it into their spirits.

8. Obey God, not tradition.

One evening the soldiers and the people in the camp wanted to have a thank-you time for us, so they invited us to join them for a special musical evening. I listened contentedly as they sat together and sang to the rhythmic, harmonic sounds of the marimbas that had somehow found their way through the jungle and into the camp.

As the music reached a happy, faster-paced tempo, some of the people who lived there stood to their feet and began to dance and clap. It was a light-hearted, forget-your-troubles, folk-type of dancing. Before I knew what was happening, a small-statured guerrilla, with a scar all across his face from where he had been knifed, grabbed my hands and pulled me to my feet. Then he stood there, smiling, swaying and shuffling his feet. Shocked out of my wits, I realized that was his way of asking me to dance with him.

How could I pull away and excuse myself without insulting him and his people? Staring blankly into his laughing eyes, in a split second I sent what seemed to be hundreds of mixed thoughts and prayers heavenward.... "God, help me! What am I supposed to do? I can't do this! I've always thought dancing was wrong. Think of all the Christians I've judged who've done it. Oh, Lord, I don't even know how to dance! How can I get myself out of this?"

Instantly, it was if God answered deep inside: "It's all right. Use this opportunity to tell this man of My love. Look straight into his eyes. Talk to him about Me. Pray for him. Let him see My love in your eyes as you `dance' with him."

I took a deep breath and a step. Then another and another. I'd never danced a step in my life, but the guerrilla didn't seem to notice. My embarrassment and awkwardness faded as the assurance filled my spirit that I was hearing God, even though what He was saying ran counter to what I'd always believed His way should be. In my heart I knew I was ministering.

Managing somehow to keep in step, I looked straight into his eyes and smiled. "I know you don't understand me," I said, "but Jesus is going to take these words and put them into your spirit. Jesus loves you more than you will ever know. He loves you so much that He even died for you. If you were the only person ever to be on Earth, Jesus would have died for you. I'm asking the Holy Spirit to speak these words to your heart in your language. Somehow, in His way and in His time, God the Father is going to let you know how much He really loves you and cares about you. If this is the only reason I came to Guatemala—so you could hear of Jesus tonight— I'm glad I came."

Then I just prayed for the man. I prayed healing upon all his memories and the hurts he had suffered. I told him how sorry I was that he hadn't had the opportunity to grow up hearing about Jesus, but that Jesus could heal him and give him an abundant, overflowing life in the midst of the poverty all around him.

When the music ended, the guerrilla smiled warmly and gave a little bow. I returned his smile and sat down, overcome by the breadth of God's holy love that becomes all things to all men that it might win some.

After that experience, I felt free to pray similar prayers with anyone to whom I felt drawn in the days ahead: soldiers, old people, widows. Somehow, in spite of all my inadequacies, I sensed that the prayers would not return void.

One day we traveled deeper into the jungle to another resettlement camp. Enduring bone-jarring jolts as we hit ruts and rocks and bottomless potholes, I rubbed my aching back with one hand and held on for dear life with the other. Picturing what I must look like bouncing along in the back of a big army truck with all these soldiers with their machine guns, I couldn't help but laugh out loud. If my mother could have seen where I was at that moment, she would have had a cardiac arrest!

At that second camp, once again I felt led to go to the people and to the soldiers, one by one, praying that they would come to know Jesus as Savior and that their lives would never be the same. I realized that obeying God sometimes meant doing something completely out of the ordinary, something outside the comfortable confines of our tradition.

9. Trust God to do exceeding abundantly beyond all you can do, ask or think (Eph. 3:20).

Even after the missions group had returned home, the precious Kekchi Indian people we'd left behind in that Guatemalan jungle remained in my mind. I saw children's upturned faces. Weary eyes hungry for hope and meaning. Bowed heads and hands folded in prayer. Lips praying to receive Jesus as Savior. And I saw the dirty, bare feet of children and women trudging over the ground in the day and tucked up underneath their bodies as they huddled near the fires in the cool night air.

On Sunday morning, I felt impressed to share my mental pictures with our congregation. I told them that only the men who worked in the jungle had shoes and that I'd love to go back and put shoes on the feet of the little children. After the service, a compassionate Christian businessman in our city, Stan Moser, wrote out a check that made the fulfillment of that dream possible. Soon a group from our church returned to Guatemala. After purchasing dozens and dozens of pairs of the sandals worn in that area, we went back to the relocation camp and placed shoes on feet that had never, ever worn shoes of any kind.

I still don't know exactly what all God wanted to accomplish in my life by directing me to a Guatemalan jungle instead of a Colorado ski lodge. But the sight of parched souls drinking in the Gospel and dirty feet walking about in new, plastic sandals made me so very glad that I'd heard and obeyed God's voice, allowing Him to do exceeding abundantly above all I could ask or think.

10. Rather than becoming frustrated over others' responses, ask God if there's anything He's wanting you to do.

In situations that are a little hard or awkward, I'm not the least bit offended if God wants to bypass me and use somebody else. I'm just not the heroine type. However, when our church participated in a Partnership Mission, joining with a church in Australia for an evangelistic outreach in their country, God taught me that He can use ordinary people, too.

A group of us had gone all over the area, passing out fliers inviting people to an evangelistic meeting and urging them to bring their lost friends. Some "lost friends" assumed we were serious and took us up on it.

At the meeting, several gang members wearing leather jackets and the Australian version of coon-skin hats sauntered in, drunk out of their minds. These were big, muscular guys in their twenties who went out into the outback and captured or killed kangaroos that were destroying crops.

I looked around and saw disgust on several of the Christian's faces because these drunk unsaved people had come in to break up the nice little evangelistic meeting we were having for lost people. This is crazy, I thought. Why did we invite sinners if we didn't want them to come?

Unfortunately, drunk people don't always behave very well in church, and these guys were no exception. They were talking loudly and goofing off while the evangelist was trying to preach. Obviously irritated, the preacher suddenly slammed his Bible shut and announced, "If you're not going to listen, I'm not going to preach!" Well, so much for that. These men hadn't come for the sermon anyway. They'd come to have a good time.

From my seat in the corner I had a pretty good view of the whole scene, and it looked like something out of movie. The Christian men, obviously disgusted, were just sitting there staring at this rough, tough gang of hoodlums breaking up the meeting. I couldn't understand why the men didn't do something. Didn't they see that they had a responsibility?

The more I looked, the more frustrated and angry I became. (It's always like that when we look at the circumstances, isn't it? We start thinking, Just look what's happening. Why don't they do something?)

All of a sudden, the Holy Spirit spoke to me and asked, "Why don't you do something?"

"Because those gang members are bigger than me!" I retorted without a moment's hesitation. "That's why I can't do something."

Since I was a woman accustomed to strong male leadership in the church, it had never dawned on me to say, "God, you see this situation. You see what is happening. Is there anything You want me to do?" And if God had said no, then all I would have had to do was sit quietly and pray. Instead, I sat there fuming and judging because I thought some men weren't doing what they were supposed to do.

"Why don't you do something?" It was that Voice again....

I surveyed the situation and sensed that the Lord seemed to be "staking out" the leader, telling me to go to him. I sighed apprehensively. The young man was huge!

Just then, I remembered that one day when Don and I were living in Chicago, I had felt led to share the love of Christ with gang members called the Black Panthers, but I was intimidated. Then I recalled having heard someone say, "If gang members are all together or grouped in two's and three's, you can never penetrate. But members of a gang seem to have little defense if they aren't banded together. If you can ever separate them and get one member off by himself, that one guy often will become like a little puppy dog." So that day on the Chicago street I had found found an opportunity to speak with one of the gang members alone. Sure enough, he'd become like a little child and I'd found it very easy to talk with him.

Encouraged by that memory and praying silently, I walked over to the big guy I believed the Lord was leading me to, looked up into his face and took him by his arm. (At that moment, I also felt the Holy Spirit take me by my arm.) "I want to talk to you," I said, tugging on his jacket. An expression of shock and surprise spread across his face. However, after only a moment's hesitation, he followed me outside. As the young man and I walked out the door, I noticed others in our group rising and being attached to different members of the gang by the Holy Spirit.

"Lord, would You tell me about this young man? Would you show me his heart?" I prayed silently. Some time before, the Lord had taught me the difference between praying for someone and praying about someone. (Praying for someone is talking to God about them, but praying about someone is giving God the opportunity to tell me about that person, if He desires.)

We walked out the door and found a place to sit down. I asked, "What's your name?" He told me, and we talked a few moments about what he did for a living. That's when I learned that he hunted kangaroos. Then, calling him by name, I said, "I don't know if you believe in God or know anything about Him, but I've been talking to God about you while we were walking out here. God told me that you're real rough, real mean on the outside, and you are the leader of this gang. God has also told me that you have some really deep hurts in your life, and that when you were a little boy you used to think about God. You would lie in bed, wondering if there really was a God. But then, through the years, you got hurt so many times, you decided God must not be real."

Tears filled his eyes and overflowed onto his cheeks. For an instant he hesitated, searching my face. Then, like a little boy, he leaned forward, laid his head on my shoulder and sobbed and sobbed and sobbed. As I continued to pray for wisdom, the Lord showed me how to explain the Gospel to him, and the young man received Jesus.

Seeing some of their team members witnessing to members of the gang, the other Christians began praying and actually prayed the drunken gang members sober. Several of them became Christians as well.

As the young man left the service that night, I put my hand on his shoulder and said, "I may never see you again, but you will always know that somewhere in the world there is at least one person praying for you by name." And I still do.

Lying in bed later that evening, I reflected on what the young man had told me about himself. He had been so damaged and hurt by men through the years, the only person who could have touched him was someone who resembled a mother. I realized that if one of the men in our group had approached him, the young man would have become very angry, or even violent.

"Lord," I prayed, "thank You for helping me get my eyes off of the logical. Thank You for helping me to stop asking, 'Why don't they do something?' and realize that You had me where I was for a reason. Thank You for reminding me to ask for Your wisdom and Your direction."

A Grateful Review

For a long time that evening I lay awake, thankfully reflecting on some of the truths the Lord had taught me during our walk together in the years since the doctor's wife had taken me to Colorado, submerged in suicidal depression and intending never to return to Waco, except perhaps for my own funeral.

I had learned that God has a plan and purpose for my life and that if I walk with Him, He is going to fulfill them. I knew it didn't matter whether or not Don did what he was supposed to do. He could not hinder the purposes of God for my life or my relationship with the Lord. God's purposes for me were going to be accomplished with or without my husband. God was going to be God.

I also knew for certain that God's purposes for my family would be completed. I didn't have to try to be a little god. The Lord could work in my husband's life and in my children's lives with or without me. But He had given me the opportunity to cooperate with Him in His purposes and to be with Him in some of the sweetest places of communion that could ever be. Whether He had me in a prison of circumstances, such as

Joseph began in, or in a palace, like Joseph wound up in, I could see Him as the sovereign Lord. The Deliverer. The Mighty God who has declared in His Word that He shall bring His will and purposes to pass.

"Lord," I prayed, I just thank You that You are giving me an opportunity to walk in a way that I've never walked before. Like the Children of Israel whom You led out of Egypt, I am not going to be led in the way that has been. Neither will You want me to do what the people where I am going have done. Thank You for desiring to do a new thing in my life. I know that Your `new thing' may be frightening. Even illogical. I just pray that when it comes, I will have the wisdom to listen for Your voice and the courage to obey."

Preparing For The Storm

God continued to allow one situation after another to come into my life, reinforcing the truths He had been teaching me. I had no way of knowing it then, but board by board, brick by brick, God was helping me build a fortress of truth upon the rock. A fortress that would help safeguard His sovereign purposes in the midst of the fierce winds and surging waters of the storm soon to burst in full force upon me.

Chapter 7

DOUBLE EXPOSURE

After the woman prayed for me in Colorado and the Holy Spirit snapped the chains of depression and hopelessness that had me bound, I returned to our home in Waco. For the next seven years I faced a daily choice. I could choose to be absorbed with my husband's sexual addiction, focusing my attention on his problems and trying in vain to change, control and manipulate him. Or I could choose to focus on building my life on the rock, allowing God to reveal what He wanted to perfect in me and cooperating with Him in His transforming work. The first three years were incredibly hard as I struggled with letting go of familiar, yet destructive, beliefs and behaviors. However, as the strong, secure structure of my peaceful new life on the rock took shape, the shanty-like existence I'd endured on the sand lost its appeal.

One week before leaving with several members of our congregation on a trip to Seoul, Korea, for a church growth conference hosted by Dr. Yonggi Cho, I went to talk with a counselor Don had been seeing who was a member of our church. Don and I had now been married 25 years, and my husband was self-destructing before my eyes. It was concern for his pain and his future—not mine—that took me to the counselor's office. I chose my words carefully. I wanted to see Don restored, not destroyed. I didn't have evidence or a list of facts I could point to in order to substantiate my "inner knowing" that my husband was involved in sexual immorality including homosexuality. I believed the counselor was aware of our situation and would want to help my husband find freedom from that bondage.

When the counselor replied, his words reached across the desk and slapped me in the face. "Your concerns about Don are totally unfounded," he said in cold, carefully measured tones. "Don does not have a problem. You do."

For a moment I just sat there, not believing that the counselor could have said what I'd heard. (I had no way of knowing that several years later we would cross paths in another state, and he would sincerely ask my forgiveness.) However, that day in his office when he placed all the blame for the problems in my marriage squarely upon my shoulders, I sensed that any attempts to argue my case or defend myself would be futile. Therefore, I brought the appointment to a close as graciously as I knew how and left his office.

A Visit To Prayer Mountain

The next week, my husband and I, along with other members of our congregation, left for our trip to Seoul, Korea. Don's mom had volunteered to stay in our home and take care of our fifteen year-old son Rod, and Amy, our sixteen year-old niece who, several months previously, had come to live with us. Our daughter Tamra was now married to a wonderful Christian young man she had met in college. Since they were expecting their first baby in three months, asking her to watch out for two high school sophomores might be too tall an order for her at that time.

One of the highlights of our trip to Korea was a visit to Prayer Mountain. As our group participated in a time of supplication and intercession, Don broke and began to weep. He had always had a heart toward God, but never before had I heard him pray with such earnestness, intensity and desperation. For over an hour I prayed and listened in quiet wonder as my husband poured out His soul before the Lord. "O, God, I long to be a clean and holy vessel," he wept. "Do whatever is necessary to totally purify my heart and my life."

Though I was certain that my husband's tears and prayers had moved the heart of God, I never dreamed the answer to his prayers would come so swiftly.

It's All Over

Don and I had driven in from the airport after our trip to Korea and a brief stopover in Hawaii. We had been home about ten minutes when the phone rang. Busy showing Don's mom, Rod and Amy the things we'd bought in Korea, I wasn't paying any attention to Don's conversation with the caller. Then I heard him say, "Sure. I'll meet you out in front of our house in ten minutes."

Ten minutes? As exhausted as he and I both were from jet lag, time changes and a see-it-all-now-because-we-may-never-get-a-chance-to-see-it-again schedule, what on earth could be so important to Don that he had to meet someone right then? It was Saturday afternoon, and Sunday was always the most demanding day of our week. Didn't he know he needed rest?

Don paced back and forth, checking his watch every minute and keeping a close eye on the driveway. Then the counselor's car pulled up in front, and Don hurried out the door.

Thirty minutes later, Don was back. Watching him make his way slowly up the sidewalk, I knew something was wrong. I can't even describe how bad my husband looked as he entered the door. "Helen," he said softly, "I need to see you in the bedroom, now."

The door closed behind us and we sat down. For a moment, Don just stared into space. Then, like the blow of an axe, the words came, sharply, swiftly, cutting our lives in half. Neatly severing everything that had happened before that Saturday in September 1985, from whatever would come thereafter.

"I have been involved in sexual perversion that includes homosexuality. The counselor I've been seeing has known about it. He said he let it slip while talking to one of the church leaders when we were in Korea. The board has already met. I will be meeting with them this afternoon and resigning before the church tomorrow. It's all over...."

Even though I'd been at least 95% certain that my husband's sexual involvement had not ceased seven years before, actually hearing him confess it to me with his own lips after vehemently denying it for years was a staggering blow. I sat there stunned, trying to comprehend it all. It was as if an ugly storm of monstrous proportions had unleashed its fury without warning. A wave of fear almost washed me off my feet, and a bolt of panic shivered down my spine. Questions pelted my mind like a cold, driving rain. What would happen to our children? Our ministry? Our marriage? Should I leave my husband? Should I file for divorce?

"I can't! I can't go through this again, Lord," my heart wailed. "This can't be happening! It's not real! It can't be!"

But it was real. And for seven long years the God of reality had been preparing me to meet just such a storm as this head-on. You don't have to let fear make you go all to pieces, I said to myself. Your peace and rest aren't dependent upon your husband, your children, the ministry, or your marriage. Your peace is totally dependent upon your relationship with God.

Rehearsed in what to do, I turned my thoughts toward Him under whose wings I had come to trust and find refuge. I could feel my heart quieting. The rain was still falling. The swirling flood waters were still rising, greedily eroding the sandy shore where once I had lived. The howling winds were still blowing and beating against me. But my house was not falling in or being swept away because it had been founded on the rock. The powerful truths God had built into me were holding fast.

Almost instinctively, a silent prayer formed and rose out of my being. "God, what do I do?"

The answer came and with it, a peace. "Stay. Stand with him."

I stood and walked over to my husband. Stooping to embrace him, I said, "I love you, and I will walk with you." I didn't know what those words meant, and that was okay. I didn't have to know. God knew. All I had to do was obey.

The thought of confessing his sin to Rod, Amy, Tamra and to his mother shattered Don. How would Rod, who had come weekly as a little boy to his daddy's office so he could help him memorize scriptures and grow up to be a godly man, react to the news that his father had been involved in sexual perversion? What would the news do to steadfast, stalwart Tamra, who had always loyally agreed to give up this or forego that in order that her dad's reputation not be damaged or his ministry hindered? What would happen to Amy, who had come to live with us in order to have the stability of an intact family? What depths of shame would our parents and families have to suffer? What about the reproach this would bring upon our precious congregation, and the stigma that other pastors, churches and Christians would have to carry? The weight of his sin was almost more than either of us could bear.

First, my husband called our son into the bedroom and broke the news. "Rod," he said as our unsuspecting teenager sat there wide-eyed, "what I have to share with you is the most difficult thing I'll ever have to tell you." Then Don told Rod about his sexual perversion and explained that he would be resigning his position at the church.

For a moment, Rod was silent. Then, with tears in his eyes, he looked Don full in the face and said, "Dad, you and Mom have loved me all these years, and I'm not going to stop loving you."

"Rod," Don reminded him, "because of the high profile of my ministry and the fact that our church is well-known in Waco, my story probably will be exposed in the papers. You may have to go through some embarrassing things at school."

Rod put his arms around Don and said, "Dad, I love you. If my friends reject me because of this, then they weren't really my friends."

Our next hurdle was to tell our daughter. Tamra and her husband Les came right over in response to our call. "Dad needs to talk to you," I said simply, ushering them into the bedroom.

I could read the concern on Tamra's face when she saw her father lying on the bed with a pillow clutched to his chest, his eyes blank and bloodshot, his hair uncombed. Oh, how my heart ached for our daughter who had seemed to idolize her father and had always striven to please him attempting to get his attention. Don's words absolutely staggered Tamra and Les, yet I marveled at the tender strength they displayed at the moment when Don needed compassion so desperately.

"I love you, Dad," said Tamra, putting her hand on Don's shoulder, "and I forgive you. Les and I will walk with you through this."

Don had hardly finished sharing with Tamra when God spoke to me: "Tell them about your sin of adultery."

"Oh, no, Lord!" I pled. "I've always preached purity to Rod and Tamra. She has idolized me. I've been a standard for her. Please, God, how much more can our children take? Haven't they been devastated enough already?" It was not that I wanted to hide my sin from my children so they would think their father was a bum and their mother was an angel. I had asked the Lord before if I should tell Tamra and Rod what I'd done, and He had never given me a freedom to share it with them. So why was He asking me to tell them now? The timing couldn't have been worse. Dumping even more upon them at a moment like this seemed so unwise. So insensitive.

Actually, as I was soon to discover, telling Tamra and Rod right then was one of the hardest and one of the most important things I could have done. God knew that an individual in our church was aware of my past sin had already brought it out into the open. While he was being interviewed by a reporter from the Dallas Morning News regarding Don's moral failure, the person mentioned that I'd had an affair seven years earlier. God knew my sin was about to be plastered right along with Don's on the front page of the Dallas Morning News and the Dallas Times Herald. He also knew the story of Don's failure would appear on the front page of the Fort Worth Star Telegram and in most Texas newspapers. A merciful God was allowing my children to hear the ugly truth first from my own lips, instead of reading it in some headline or hearing it told as gossip.

Though I knew none of that at the time, I did know that I must obey God. I told them.

Telling the Church

Tamra, Les, Rod and I had chosen to stand on either side of Don Sunday evening when he stood behind the pulpit, confessed his sin and presented his resignation to our 2,000-plus-member congregation. As I rose to make my way up the steps to join my husband behind the podium, I glanced up into the solemn, expressionless faces of the church leaders and staff members seated on the platform behind him. None of them were shouting accusations or hurling stones. Yet, for just an instant, I felt as if I knew how the woman taken in adultery must have felt as she was brought before Jesus, for I, too, was guilty.

As Don began to speak, haltingly, brokenly, I fought back a blur of tears and looked into the hurt, bewildered faces of the people we had betrayed by our sin. The girl attending Baylor University whom I had counseled. Women I'd taught in my Sunday school class. Elderly people who had treated me as if I were their very own daughter. Teenagers, singles, young married couples who had looked to us as their role models. I stood before those precious people, more fully aware than any of them how grievously my husband and I had violated our office of sacred trust.

As Don ended his confession to the congregation, God spoke to my heart and said, "You, too."

Stepping to the microphone, I confessed my sin and asked the people's forgiveness. Satan could never again whisper threats of exposure to me over my hidden sins. Somehow I made it through the remainder of the service.

The Media

From that evening on, the nightmare intensified. Don's letter of resignation was released to the local newspaper which in turn released it to the Associated Press. The media, like hungry cats after helpless mice, pursued us relentlessly.

Neither Don nor I had really slept since returning from Hawaii. We were physically exhausted and emotionally devastated, yet we couldn't even find a quiet corner to grieve.

Our home was turning into Grand Central Station, the switchboard at Southwestern Bell and the center-ring attraction at Barnum and Bailey's Circus—all rolled into one. A Dallas newspaper reporter tromped across our lawn, interrogating our neighbors and trying to interview us. Phones rang. Television cameras, blinding lights, media people and microphones in our faces. One reporter even called at 1:30 a.m. one night, under the pretense of an emergency, hoping Don would talk.

Once the Associated Press picked up the story, it spread faster than the Asian flu. (This was before the sins of big-name ministers such as Jim Bakker and Jimmy Swaggart were exposed, so a story on the moral failures of a pastor and his wife was newsy indeed.) We had never dreamed that the news would spread so far or so fast. Trying to notify as many of his close relatives as possible, Don made phone call after phone call even though he was so shattered by all the publicity that he literally could not get out of bed.

In spite of our efforts, many of our relatives were broadsided by the story before we had a chance to explain or warn them. My brother, who lived over 350 miles away, saw a headline on the front page of the newspapers he was helping get ready for his son to deliver: "Waco Pastor Resigns Over Homosexual Involvement." He thought, Hmmm. That's where Don and Helen live. I'll read that. My brother was dumbstruck to read that Don Crossland was that pastor. Concerned relatives called my mom after reading the story. "The newspaper said Helen had an affair. How could they print such trash? We know her. Why, Helen would never do such a thing!"

The day after Don resigned, people from the local television station came unannounced into our house and did an interview with me. I had stumbled over something, ripped off a toenail and couldn't even wear my shoes. But when you've already lost your reputation and your job, and your very soul has been laid bare before the world, hobbling around barefooted in front of reporters and television cameras is your least concern.

I earnestly committed the interview to the Lord, and He gave me an incredible peace. As the reporter asked one probing question after another, I knew God was giving me the right words to say. The interview was drawing to a close when I felt compassion welling up inside for the man interviewing me. I began praying about him to the Lord, asking God to reveal the reporter's needs and help me minister to him.

"He's not involved in church, and he doesn't have a close relationship with Me," the Lord said. "When he was a little boy he had a deep interest in spiritual things and felt My call upon his life. Even now he sometimes lies on his bed, thinking about how much I meant in his life when he was little and wondering if the things he believed about Me as a child were really true."

As soon as the cameras and microphones were turned off and the crew was busy packing up, I quietly shared with the man what the Lord had said. As I spoke, he kept nodding in agreement. Visibly moved by his sudden awareness of God's love and concern for him, the reporter told me that the words I had spoken were true. Through that simple occurrence God assured me that even in our times of deepest distress He can minister through us to others.

The Ripple Effect

If my husband and I were staggering from the impact of our sins' exposure upon our church, friends and loved ones, I could only imagine the pain and shame that Tamra and Rod must be experiencing. From the very first, Rod hid his pain behind a brave, funny front. It would be years later that we would begin to see the effect in Tamra's life.

The Sunday night of Don's resignation, Rod took a look at my forlorn face as we drove up to the church a few minutes before time for the evening service. "Mom," he asked, trying to cheer me up, "does this mean we've lost our reserved parking place?" We both broke into nervous laughter.

That next week at school, Rod began experiencing even more "fall-out" as truths, half-truths and rumors circulated wildly among his peers and teachers. One evening as Tamra and Rod were chatting. I happened to overhear part of their conversation.

"I think I'm going to get a new wardrobe," remarked Rod nonchalantly.

"Why? Are you wanting to change your self-image?"

"No, I'd like to change my identity."

I winced, sensing the pain and embarrassment Rod must be feeling.

The next day as Rod came walking in the door, I asked, "How was school?"

"Well," he replied with a dimpled grin, "when they called the roll and said `Rod Crossland' I answered `Here.' But I almost said, `That's my name, but I go by Robert White now.'"

I chuckled sympathetically, through I wanted to cry.

"Mom," asked Rod with a half-hearted smile, "do they give group rates for name changes?"

Later, Rod saw me break down and sob as the story of Don's sexual perversion and my infidelity was smeared across the pages of practically every newspaper in Texas. He patted me sympathetically on the shoulder. "Don't cry, Mom," he said. "Just think...in a couple of years you can sell this as a soap opera and make lots of money!"

Sin Versus Repentance

At the time I had plunged recklessly into the affair, I'd thought it was my business and I could do what I pleased. Later, I learned that we never sin without someone else being affected, for our sin sets certain spiritual laws in motion.

On the other hand, God made me to know that the reverse of that law holds true, as well: Just as we cannot sin without affecting others, neither can we repent without affecting others. Repenting and getting right with God releases tremendous power and anointing in our own lives and in the lives we touch.

Thank God for the transforming process of repentance and restoration. Thank God that out of weakness we can be made strong. Thank God for His amazing grace.

Chapter 8

THE NIGHT OF WIND AND FIRE

That first week after my husband's resignation seemed like one unending nightmare. Early one morning before the sun came up or the phone began its incessant ringing I slipped out of bed, careful not to awaken Don, and made my way to a quiet corner of the house where I could pray without being interrupted or disturbing anyone else. Oh, how I needed to hear from God and receive His grace and wisdom for the approaching day.

A burden for my husband was especially heavy on my heart that morning. I remembered all too well the crushing weight of shame and hopelessness that had plunged me into suicidal depression seven years before. I shuddered at the thought of Don experiencing a similar nightmare. What was I supposed to do? How could I help him? How should I pray for him?

I told the Lord that I didn't know or understand a lot of things about my husband. I asked the Holy Spirit to release me from the limitations of my natural mind and understanding, give me divine wisdom and show me Don's heart.

As I continued praying, a strange thing happened. I found myself picturing Don as an infant. It was as if I could sense what he was sensing and feel what he was feeling, yet I was able to verbalize to myself what he as a baby could not.

I saw Don lying all alone in his crib hour after hour, day after day. When a kiss or cuddle came it was so quick, the emotionally starved baby's need for nurturing and affection was never met. When he was fed or diapered, the job was taken care of quickly and accompanied by a very tired, worn-out voice. There was no leisurely rocking and holding the baby snugly in secure, loving arms. Just lying in his crib, silently scanning the walls and ceiling for a friendly face. Listening intently for a caring voice. Needing to be touched and fed and loved. Wondering why no one came. Feeling alone. Abandoned. Rejected. I asked Don's mother about it later and, with pain-filled eyes, she told me it was true. She also described her plight to Don and asked his forgiveness. She shared with us how she had been a harried, exhausted, 23-year-old at the time, and Don had been her fifth child. She already had a 1-year-old, a 2-year-old, a 3-year-old and a 4-year-old clamoring for her attention. Just before she got pregnant with Don, her physical condition was so poor the doctor had warned her that having another baby could kill her. The doctor had advised her to have an abortion - for her health's sake. (Abortion had not been legalized at that time.)

That morning after I wept for Don as a helpless, neglected baby, the picture and feelings gradually faded, only to be followed by other images and emotions. The Lord let me experience the anguish and rejection my husband felt when he was 5 years old and heard his father arguing with his mom, saying Don wasn't his son and calling him a bastard.

I felt what Don felt as a little boy when, terrified by a thunderstorm, he tiptoed into his parents' bedroom and quietly crawled into bed beside his father. I felt his shock and despondency when his father kicked him out of bed onto the cold hardwood floor, ordering him to stop being a sissy and act like a man.

God let me feel the emotions my husband experienced when his parents left him with his great-aunt summer after summer.... Trying to figure out why none of his brothers or sisters ever went with him, wondering why somebody didn't come to get him and take him home when he got homesick. I felt my husband's shame and hurt as he stood at the window watching his father and brothers while they piled into the truck to go fishing after he had been ordered to stay home and iron clothes. I felt his pain and silent rage as he was made to wash dishes while his brothers relaxed or did the chores classified as "man's work."

I felt Don's fright and distress at the age of 17 when his father cursed him and forced him to leave home with only $17 in his pocket and no place to go. I grieved at the thought of him having to check into a sleazy motel that first night, then lying in bed and sobbing until morning.

I recalled little things my husband had shared about witnessing sexual experimentation among other males during his teenage years. Although he did not participate, Don longed for the closeness they seemed to find with each other. It was then that he had begun to believe the lie that male closeness involves some degree of sexual intimacy.

I don't know how long I knelt there that morning, weeping and praying for my husband. I had just seen him in a totally different light. Physically he was a mature man, and when it came to spiritual knowledge, Don was very mature, as well. But emotionally, my husband was not mature. Inside, he was still a damaged, rejected little boy. When my sobs finally subsided, I went to Don and described what had happened. "How many people have ever come to you asking how you hurt, what you've felt, or inviting you to share your heart?" I asked.

"No one...." he answered softly, looking away. "No one in my entire life."

I sat beside my husband, bewildered and stunned. Not one person or group from our church family came to either of us with those questions. Nor had even one Christian asked to lay hands on Don and pray for his deliverance. Why? I could understand why the handful of people who had reached out and tried to restore Don seven years before, after his sin had been exposed to them along with my own moral failure, might feel like washing their hands of him. After all, they had given him one chance back then, and he had broken his promises to them and become involved in sexual perversion once more. They weren't experienced counselors in sexual addiction. They did not know that, almost without exception, every individual coming out of addiction will go through another near failure or fall on the road to full recovery.

But what about all the other people who wrote my husband off as a loss the instant they learned of his moral failure? It just didn't make sense to me. If Don's problem had been in the physical realm—a heart attack or a disease such as cancer, for instance— believers would have come to him and offered prayer. But since his problem was in the moral and spiritual realm, it seemed easier for people simply to turn their backs and walk away.

Physician, Heal Thyself

Don and I had done a lot of talking in the past few days. I thought of the people from whom my husband said he had sought help through the years.... There was the psychiatrist in Washington who saw Don and then told me that if I wanted to help my husband, I should resign myself to the fact that he would always be involved in bisexual behavior. There were the therapists who had reluctantly admitted their powerlessness to help someone bound to addictive patterns; the psychiatrist who leaned back in his chair, closed his eyes and began to snore right in the middle of Don's third (and final) session with him; and the counselors who secretly acknowledged their own bondage to life-controlling problems....

I still had to shake my head in disbelief when I thought about my husband's appointment with a Catholic priest who had a reputation for counseling people in sexual addiction. After listening to Don's confession, the priest had confided that he had the same problem. Then he shared several precautions Don should begin taking to avoid being exposed and losing his place of ministry. Certain that a counselor who hadn't found a solution for his own sexual addiction couldn't tell another addict how to be freed, Don had walked out of the man's office and never returned.

I bowed my head and wept. I'd heard Don's prayers. I'd seen his tears. I knew he was crying out to God for help, pleading to be purified and delivered. Was there no help for my husband? Could the chains binding him to his addictive sinful patterns be broken, or was Don doomed to be enslaved to an endless cycle of sin, denial and shame for the rest of his life?

Holy, Healing Fire

One night about a week after Don's resignation I noticed he seemed very restless and uncomfortable. "Helen," he finally asked, "do I have fever?"

"No," I said, touching his forehead, "I don't think so. Why? Do you feel sick?"

"No.... I...I just feel strange, that's all. Like I'm on fire inside," Don replied, rubbing his chest. "And I keep hearing this whirling, roaring sound.... Like wind, or something.... Do you hear it?"

"You're probably just really tired, Don," I said, trying to reassure him. "You've been under such extreme pressure."

But an hour or so later, my husband came to me again and asked me to take his temperature. "I'm sure I must have fever," he said once again, rubbing his chest. "I still feel so hot inside, as if I'm burning up. And that sound.... It's like a whirlwind...."

This time I used a thermometer, just to make sure. "No," I said, "you don't have fever. I don't know what's wrong, but try to get some sleep. You should feel better in the morning."

Don slept fitfully almost all night long, tossing and turning, rubbing his chest, repeating that he felt as if he were on fire and heard a whirling sound. Finally, as morning dawned, he fell into a deep, sound sleep.

When my husband awoke, something was different. The whirling noise and the burning sensation inside had disappeared. But it was more than that.... Almost afraid to move lest he disturb the uncanny sense of unfettered peace inside, Don sat up and looked around. The truth took a moment to register.... God had done it. A miracle had occurred. He was free from a demonic stronghold! For the first time that he could recall in his life, he didn't feel the sucking vacuum from what he had described as a huge chasm in his soul—a vacuum that had created an almost insatiable need to be nurtured or touched.

The minute Don told me I knew it was true. I had not heard the whirlwind. I had not felt God's holy fire. But I sensed something else just as real. The dark, evil presence that had forced its way into our home back in Washington years before was gone! We weren't existing under its oppressive shadow. The thing—which I called a "spirit of perversion"— was no longer dogging Don's every step. The very atmosphere in our home had changed. The feeling was as real as if an unwelcome, uninvited visitor who had lived with us for years had suddenly gathered up his belongings and disappeared in the night without a trace. Indeed, that is exactly what had happened.

Believing our problems were over, I was so relieved and excited. I didn't yet understand that a deliverance in the spirit is not the same as restoration of the soul. I'd never heard that the word "restoration," as used in Galations 6:1, means a process, not a quick-fix. Neither did I know that deliverance can be instantaneous, but restoration almost always takes time. If transformation is to take place, the mind must be renewed.

Living Proof

Don knew he had been delivered. I knew he had been delivered. But would other people ever be convinced of that fact? I saw certain individuals literally hating Don and refusing to believe that he had repented, and I longed so desperately for them to see and believe. But how do you convince people of the reality of something they haven't seen or experienced for themselves? If only there were some sort of before-and-after spiritual "x-rays" that people like my husband could hold up and say, "See, that dark spot right there? That was my problem. Now, look at this picture taken of the identical area one week later. See? The dark spot is gone!"

As I pursued that wishful line of reasoning I said to myself, "Yeah, then we would be in the same dilemma confronted by people who testify to sceptics that they've been healed of cancer. The sceptics say, 'Oh, is that so? Well, I won't believe it unless I see the doctor's x-rays.' So the individuals produce the x-rays, and the sceptics retort, 'Aw, there must have been a mistake made somewhere. Either those aren't really your x-rays, or you never had cancer in the first place. I still don't believe you were healed.'"

I knew the bottom line for my husband and me was: Who were we supposed to be trying to please and obey, anyway? Men, who look only upon the outward appearance, or God, who looks on the heart?

Besides, after the experience I'd had in prayer a few days earlier when I'd seen Don as an infant, a child and a young man and felt the indescribable pain and sense of rejection he had felt much of his life, I knew much healing work would still have to take place before my husband would experience more degrees of wholeness. However, as difficult as that process might be, one wonderful truth now radiated in our hearts, its brilliant, unwavering light shining upon the path before us: Don had repented and been miraculously delivered from a spirit of sexual perversion. Its iron-tight grip on our lives had been broken. We had already passed the first giant hurdle on our journey toward wholeness.

Chapter 9

YE WHO ARE SPIRITUAL....

Aware that Don and I must be totally exhausted (we were) and that we needed a reprieve from the merciless bombardment of the media, our friend Jack Taylor invited us to use his family's vacation condominium on the Florida beach to get away for a while. By this time, my husband didn't have physical strength to drive that distance, and I was running on the last reserves of my own. I was praying that God would help me and give supernatural strength to stay awake while driving. Within only a few hours of leaving a friend volunteered to drive our family part of the way so Don and I could rest.

When we stopped at Jack and Barbara's house in Ft. Worth to get the key to the condominium, there on the doorstep lay a newspaper with the headline: "Waco Pastor Quits Because of Homosexuality." My husband clutched his chest, and his face twisted in agony. For a moment, I thought he'd had a heart attack. Then I saw the paper.

A friend of ours who was ministering in Little Rock, Arkansas, had asked us to come through there on our way to Florida so he could pray for us. We were so starved for any crumb of acceptance, we didn't consider the trip to Little Rock to be out of our way. Our friend's sensitive, sincere prayer touched our hearts and ministered to us. (Only much later did he dare tell us that it was the "least-faithed" prayer he had ever prayed.)

Our friend who had been driving us flew back home from Little Rock, leaving Rod, Amy, Don and I to continue our lonely journey to Florida. As usual, with Rod and Amy we couldn't get totally self-focused. The two of them laughed and teased, deliberately confusing Don on their orders at every fast-food restaurant we stopped at along the way.

Finally, we reached our destination. After being confined in the van for so many hours, it felt good to unpack and wander about the lovely condominium. The calendar might have read "Sunday," but it certainly didn't feel anything like the Sunday mornings to which our family was accustomed. I couldn't even imagine how hard it must have been for Don to be sitting there with "just us" when he was used to preaching before large congregations in three morning services each Sunday. Ironically, that very Sunday the church had planned to expand to four services in order to accommodate the crowds. I wondered how many, many more painful changes lay ahead for us.

Time to Think

Getting away from the bedlam of ringing telephones and brash reporters gave us space to breathe and time to think. And when I had time to think, I discovered that in spite of the miraculous deliverance my husband had already experienced, painful memories from our troubled marriage had doggedly followed me to Florida. I found myself rehearsing many hurts from the past: Don did this and this and this to me...and this and this and this! I could leave him now, and no one would blame me. Why, even Don's own mother has told me she will certainly understand if I leave and that she will always love me like a daughter, regardless of what I do.... My confused thoughts kept turning round and round like a dog chasing its tail. Oh, how I struggled.

But even as I contemplated the past and a future that looked very, very bleak, I could not get away from another voice inside: Hear God, and walk in obedience. Hear God, and walk in obedience. The Lord had told me to stay and walk with Don. I knew that God knew best, and that I would obey.

A Promise of Hope

That Sunday afternoon, Don went for a walk on the beach by himself. When he told me about it later, the words came tumbling out. "At that point, I was so weighed down by my failure and the reproach I'd brought upon my family and congregation, I had no desire to live or to minister again. I felt so ashamed of my actions, I wished I could hide away in some isolated cave and become a nameless hermit, or muster the nerve to walk out into the ocean and never return. As lonely and miserable as my life as a child had been, I wished I'd never left the farm where I grew up. I wished I'd never stood behind a pulpit and preached. What was I going to do with my life now? How was I going to make a living for my family—if I still had a family—when all this was over?"

Don blinked back the tears and cleared his throat, determined to tell it all. "I finally just stopped, right out there on the sand and asked, `God, am I an example of Your judgment?' I hadn't expected an answer, but to my surprise, one came back. The words were so clear and precise, they stunned me. God said, `You will be an example of My mercy, grace and restoration.' "

My husband broke and began to weep. I wept with him. God had given us a word of hope to which we could cling in the perplexing years ahead.

Confronting Reality

In Florida, Don and I talked about how much we were looking forward to returning to Waco, choosing the least conspicuous seats in the church auditorium and beginning our healing process. We clung to a statement our church leaders had released to the newspapers stating that they did not believe the wounded should be shot, but restored. Don and I never expected to minister there again as pastors, of course. It was just that the people were like family to us, and we felt such a need to be among them. We knew it would be awkward and painful for all of us at first, but the people seemed so strong and stable, we believed just sitting among them and worshipping with them would help us heal.

Our days on the peaceful Florida coast quickly drew to an end. We knew we had to go home and face reality, brutal as it might be. As Don drove us home, I thought a lot about God's word to him: "You will be an example of My mercy, grace and restoration." I knew that God's power and His purpose were far greater than I could imagine, yet I also sensed that we would have many miles of desolate wilderness to cross before we reached the place of restoration God had promised. I comforted myself with the thought that at least we would be in the presence of friends whose wisdom and understanding could help guide us along our difficult path. That, however, was not to be.

Don't Come Back

We drove back into Waco early Saturday morning. I had unpacked our suitcases and had begun tackling the mountain of dirty clothes from our trip when the doorbell rang. Two of the church leaders stood at our door. One look at their solemn, anxious faces as we invited them inside sent a shiver of apprehension down my back.

Haltingly, they passed on the message they had been sent to deliver. "Some of the members doubt your repentance, Don," they explained. "Others believe you're genuinely sorry, but they've been deeply wounded by your sin. The people need time to work through their anger and their sense of having been betrayed. They need time to heal. We're asking you not to return to the church at all at this time or talk to any of the members. "

The leaders also informed us that Don's name had been removed from the church's membership. I asked them to remove mine, too.

We tried to be understanding and gracious, but after they left, one look at my husband's weary face told me that he felt as forsaken and heavyhearted as I did. Don and I held each other and wept. Recalling the church leaders' statement we'd read in the paper about ministering to the wounded rather than shooting them, I couldn't help feeling as if the wounded had been shot, abandoned and left to bleed to death.

"I feel so alone," Don sighed. "So isolated. Don't they understand how much our whole family needs them right now?"

Once again, words that I'd found myself saying a lot over the past few years worked their way to the surface. "Don, I know it's wrong, but it's right." I could tell that my husband resented the statement and didn't understand what it meant, but at that moment I was saying it as much for my own benefit as for his. I needed to remind myself that God can use even what we may think are wrong circumstances to work out what is right for us and for others.

By late that afternoon, Don was able to view our situation from a different perspective. "Some things may seem wrong and unjust," he sighed, "but in reality God is preparing us for the things He has for us in the future. He is using this situation, as painful as it might be, to develop qualities in us that we wouldn't acquire otherwise."

Wounded Shepherd, Wounded Sheep

After he'd had a lot more time to reflect upon the leaders' request that we not come back to the church, Don explained it to me even more clearly. "You and I have been wounded through all of this, and the people have all been wounded, too. Wounded sheep cannot be healed by a wounded shepherd. Neither can a wounded flock help us heal." My husband paused, giving what he'd just said time to sink in.

"The people we've pastored need to experience healing from Jesus Himself. Like ours, their healing is going to take time. Our presence in the congregation could create confusion and division, and it would prolong the healing process for all of us. Even though this leaves you and me wandering around out in the wilderness by ourselves, it will have been better for all of us in the end."

Wilderness Lessons

Though neither Don nor I understood at the time how such a thing would ever be, that Saturday night as he lay in bed dreading another Sunday away from our church family, the Holy Spirit assured my husband once more that the leaders' decision was right. God made Don to know that He had a different plan for his life and a new direction for him.

The Lord brought Hosea 2:14 to my husband's mind: "I will allure her, bring her into the wilderness and speak kindly to her." As he meditated upon that verse and the verses surrounding it, Don recognized that not only had his ministry become the basis of his identity and self-worth, it had become a god to him: Now his god had been stripped from him. God would use his wilderness experience to remove him further from the source of his idolatry and to lure him back to Himself, just as He had done with the idolatrous children of Israel.

Neither of us were interested in a trek through some barren desert. Yet as much as we dreaded a "wilderness" experience, Don felt an assurance deep in his heart that the period of probation or "exile" ahead would not destroy us or God's ministry for us. Instead, he believed it would help bring him to deeper repentance and greater maturity and would mold and strengthen his character so he could have a more fulfilling life and fruitful ministry.

Struggles of My Own

While my husband was searching for answers, I was having a few struggles of my own As clearly as I can recall, Don's mother was the only person during those first few weeks who supported my decision to stay with Don. Most of the people in the church simply took it for granted that my husband and I would divorce.

The week we returned from Florida, I was invited to lunch by a woman in the church. "Helen," she said, "you know, of course, that you have scriptural grounds for leaving your husband. You are free to divorce him."

I responded gently. "If God speaks that to me, I'm free to obey it. So far, He has said for me to stay and walk with Don."

"But, Helen!" she protested. "The number of people who truly repent and break free of sexual perversion once and for all is minimal. How many do you know who have? These people just don't change."

"You've got to stop protecting Don, Helen. You have yourself and your children to think of. Face the facts. You can either divorce him, or you can die with AIDs—if you don't starve first. Don is a preacher, yet in all probability he will never preach again. How does he plan to make a living for you? By working at a service station pumping gas? Your only hope is to get out, get a divorce and find a better life."

I could not hold back the tears. My soul agreed with her. Only weeks before I had seriously struggled with the thought that I had to get out of the marriage in order to really live."I know what you're saying," I replied, "and I've wrestled with those very issues. But God has told me to stay, and unless He tells me otherwise, my safest recourse is to obey Him."

I never doubted for a moment that the woman sincerely cared about me as a person and was genuinely interested in my welfare. As a matter of fact, she was the only person I can recall who had reached out to me at that time with advice of any kind. Although I'd taught a women's Sunday school class for years and had led the women's ministries program at our church, I now felt abandoned and isolated. That fact was a source of disappointment to me, but I realized that I had disappointed many of those people, too. This woman, on the other hand, had invited me to lunch and addressed an issue of tremendous importance and sensitivity.

I respected her courage and appreciated her concern.

That person's mind-set and that of the church leadership seemed to be mirror images of one another. "Helen," they reasoned firmly, "your sin was not right, but all that Don put you through makes it more understandable. In addition, these past seven years have borne witness to your genuine repentance and restoration. If you divorce Don, the church will help take care of you and your family. However, if you choose to stay with your husband, there's nothing more we can do than what we've already discussed with Don—three month's salary and some counseling, should he desire it."

I did not believe that those men were trying to be insensitive or mean. As I learned afterward, they were simply following standard procedures for handling immorality in the ministry—standards that are approved and employed widely to this day in several large denominations.

One well-meaning church leader bought a book to see how to deal with my husband's sin. After reading it, he came to us and said, "This is what so and so in such and such a place did. I believe this is what you should do, too." As the man talked with my husband and me, advising us to follow the exact steps the person in the book had taken, I grew even more convinced that we Christians dare not base our dealings with one another solely upon a pattern God gave someone else for a similar situation.

I also had become equally convinced that, ideally, when Christians meet as a body of believers in order to take counsel together and reach a decision, our purpose should not be to determine the mind of the majority but the mind of the Holy Spirit—something which may be quite different.

Recognizing early on that majority rule is not necessarily any sign of God's leadership in a situation, I had taught many times about the 12 men mentioned in Numbers 13 who were sent to spy out the land. Ten of the 12 came back relating the dangers and apparent futility of attempting to possess it. However, they had totally missed the point. God hadn't sent them into the land in order to decide whether or not they should possess it. God had already decided that for them. He just wanted them to see the land and determine how they should prepare and strategize for the warfare that would be necessary to tear it from the grasp of the enemy.

More Disappointments

We had lost our ministry and our church home, but it didn't take long to realize that our losses didn't end there. I don't know what we would have done had it not been for the precious handful of people who ministered love and encouragement to us in their special ways.... The man who regularly brought hand-written scriptures to our door. The woman who asked me to lunch. The older woman who dropped by once a week for a visit. The small group who realized that Don and I had no service to attend and began coming to our home on Wednesday evenings to encourage us. Such people were a rare exception, and they ministered to us more than they could know.

Most people we had considered would be friends for life suddenly no longer spoke to us. Many times we waited until after midnight to go grocery shopping just so we could avoid being seen. I dreaded going to the grocery store because individuals I'd known for years now turned and hurried down another aisle rather than face me. When one woman saw me coming up the aisle toward her, she literally left her shopping cart and ran out of the store. Sometimes, when such things happened I felt anger, but mostly I just felt pity and disappointment. When I found myself wanting to judge those whom I believed were judging us, the Holy Spirit tenderly reminded me that judging was judging. That's all it took to remind me that I wanted no part of passing judgment on anybody. Frankly, I wasn't all that sure that I might not have reacted just as those believers did, had our roles been reversed.

And then there were the petty, but hurtful, annoyances such as not receiving our mail for several days because some anonymous person contacted the post office and told them we had moved. There were also many rumors and false accusations.

One day after still another false accusation concerning my husband had been relayed to us by phone, it was if a light popped on in my head. I looked at Don and exclaimed, "I've got it! I know what is happening." Mentioning another minister's name, I said, "He's very similar to you in both size and appearance. If someone was not fairly well acquainted with both of you, it would be very easy to get you confused with one another. Just think about this for a moment," I continued. "The same lies we keep hearing about you are the same stories that others have related to us in the past about the other minister. Remember the young person who came to us and asked if we would confront the minister about the drug and pornography parties he was having at his home? The individual said that the minister's small church was only a front to cover his activities." (Several years later when we learned that the minister died amid mysterious circumstances, I couldn't help but wonder if he had felt as addicted and hopeless as Don had been.)

As Don and I continued to discuss my theory of mistaken identity in regard to the rumors circulating about him, Don mentioned a remark that had been made to him on several occasions. "If only you had just committed adultery, that sin could be understood and forgiven. But not homosexuality."

I nodded. "When it comes to understanding the depth and breadth of God's mercy and forgiveness, I'm afraid that the church in general has more problems than we've ever thought."

"You know, Helen," my husband said, "sin is sin. The way I look at it, the sins of the minister you mentioned are no blacker than ours. The steel-jawed grip of addiction lured and pulled me right into a cesspool of activity, so what does it matter if I get blamed for more than I did? Personally, if I had a choice, I'd prefer to have people think the worst about us and then see them find out that they were wrong than to believe that things weren't nearly as bad as they were, then discover that much more was actually involved. In a way, I almost feel a strange sense of relief as far as the rumors about me are concerned."

After that conversation I realized that I was beginning to feel really free inside. One day I found myself thinking, This is a blessing in disguise. I can't get kicked out of anything, because I don't belong to anything. I can't lose my reputation, because it's already lost. I am finally free to find out and be who I really am. For the first time in my life, my identity is not wrapped up in anyone or in anything. Discovering who the real me was and who she would turn out to be might prove to be an interesting journey after all.

Blessed Are the Merciful

I'd never realized that there is more to restoration than simply stopping sinful behavior. Neither had I understood that, although God can enable us to do anything we have to do if no one is around to help us, ideally, we should not be forced to try all alone to bring restoration to ourselves. We desperately need the help of brothers and sisters in Christ who can come alongside us to help bear our burdens, minister correction and healing, pray with and for us and hold us accountable spiritually. Paul understood this principle and instructed the Galatians: "Brethren, if a man is overtaken in any trespass, you who are spiritual restore such a one in a spirit of gentleness, considering yourself lest you also be tempted" (6:1, NKJV).

Just when our future looked hopeless and Don and I were feeling utterly abandoned, a group of Christian leaders together committed themselves to seeing my husband restored. As far as Don and I are concerned, their names, forever imprinted upon our hearts, are synonymous with Christian compassion, faithfulness and mercy: James Robison. Rick Godwin. Peter Lord. Clark Whitten. Dudley Hall. Dick King. Jack Taylor. They never failed to return a phone call. They never refused our requests to see them and sit down and talk with them when we needed to. When our salary from the church stopped after three months, some of those men underwrote our financial support for the next year. When a former offer for counseling did not materialize, they made it possible for my husband and me to pay for counseling.

After Don's resignation as a pastor, God gave us respectively, Rick Godwin, Jack Taylor, Jamie Buckingham and Dick King as our pastors. These men were committed to us and played critical roles in Don's restoration.

Our faithful friends continued to stand with us and our board members thankfully, did not resign, but very patiently waited as we worked through our confusion. Other precious brothers and sisters in Christ also provided blessing and encouragement along the way. In spite of the risk of rejection, several of the people we had pastored began reaching out to us.

Some believers called my husband to encourage him. Others took us into their homes for the weekend. Some had us join them for their church services. One minister, who stands out in our minds as an example of compassion and mercy, invited us out to dinner and treated us like very special people.

When my husband and I felt like lepers, these people dared to reach out to us. Not put off by the fact that we had become untouchable outcasts in the spiritual community, they took us into their hearts and made room for us in their lives. Shouldering the burdens we could not carry alone, they walked along beside us during some of the most treacherous, difficult miles of our journey toward wholeness. We will forever be grateful.

Chapter 10

HE RESTORETH MY SOUL

Exposure and repentance were only part of the process of restoration—not the entire thing. To stop there would have set Don up for another relapse. He had so seared a part of his conscience and so compartmentalized his life that somehow he had been able, in his deception and rationalization, to keep the sinful, shame-ridden part of his life from integrating with other parts. Now he began to ask the Holy Spirit to help him work through every aspect of his problem with sexual perversion.

In his book, Refocusing Your Passions, Don relates how hurts rooted deeply in his past had to be searched out and healed. He tells how harmful behavior patterns had to be recognized, dismantled and replaced by righteous, healthy ones. He explains how new boundaries, with accountability, needed to be established.1

In addition to all of those things that had to be dealt with, a recurring nightmare had begun plaguing my husband. At times he was running from something, terror-stricken. Other times he was totally immobilized by fear. Each time he awoke in a cold sweat. Finally, we realized that these specific dreams were important and that long-buried memories were trying to surface. (Repressed memories are different from memories relating to false memory syndrome.)

At last, the faded, blurred memories began to sharpen and focus. Their revelations shocked and disturbed my husband, but they also taught both of us even more about him. As the closed compartment slowly opened and healing continued, Don's conscious mind began accepting what earlier it couldn't, being molested when he was five or six years old by a farm worker. Then he remembered being molested again at age seven by a laborer who worked for his father. Later, my husband also recalled how an older neighborhood boy had tried to molest him while they were playing in Don's father's garage when he was even younger. He remembered how frightened he had been as the boy struck matches, threatening to burn him if Don did not submit to his sexual demands. I could feel the terror he felt when the garage caught on fire and burned down and his father blamed him for the accident.

Deep in our hearts, Don and I knew we desperately needed expert Christian counseling to help us work through it all. Our savings were dwindling fast, but the group of Christian leaders who were underwriting our salary also made it possible for us to seek out and pay for counseling. Only God knew what that would mean to us and our future.

Don, You're An Addict.

We were both extremely nervous during our first three-and-a-half-hour drive to visit the psychotherapist who had been recommended to us. After some of our previous experiences with counselors, we were apprehensive, to say the least.

But from the moment we entered this counselor's office, my husband and I both sensed that this woman was different. She was gracious and attentive, easy to talk to and extremely competent. We felt God's presence and love in her warm, confident manner.

As we shared our story the counselor listened intently. I could tell that Don felt at ease in her presence. He related that he had never known a time when he had not felt an emptiness and a dark hole, inside. He shared that for years he had felt unworthy and isolated and had never allowed others, even me, to be deeply involved in his life.

My husband explained that, through his college days and the early years of our marriage, he had questioned this emotional void, but eventually had come to accept it as normal. He shared that he had attempted to fill the void and ease the pain in unhealthy ways since he had come to feel that he could not trust God to heal his wounds and fill the void. He admitted that his immoral behavior could have been an attempt to deal with the emptiness he felt inside. However, the more he had continued in that cycle of sin and death, the greater his feeling of loneliness and his separation from God and others intensified. Don confided that many times he would lay face down on the floor of his office sobbing and crying out to God to fill the awful emptiness and loneliness he felt inside.

As the session continued and my husband began sharing details of his past behavior, the counselor looked him straight in the eyes and said softly, "Don, you're an addict." Then she explained that most addictions are a search for a relationship—an attempt to fill a void or repair an emotional wound from years past. She helped us understand that his fear of abandonment and hurt was a lingering sickness from years of emotional wounds and molestations. She explained that being molested had made him feel ashamed, hidden and afraid to be open.

Neither of us liked the word "addict." Even though he had stopped acting out sexually, we knew the counselor was right and that we needed help in working through the pain of the past. Long before that first session was over, my husband had decided that he would stick with the therapy no matter how long it took. Knowing that God hadn't finished surfacing junk in my own life, I made the same commitment. (The actual time wound up being a year and a half.) Don and I found that we both had such deep hurts from our pasts that we had to be healed as individuals before we could give a thought to having a healthy marriage.

Our Father

Under the counselor's direction, my husband learned to deal with the pain and rejection he had felt from his father. One day my husband came to me and said, "Helen, I feel as if there's a volcano of emotion inside me. I need to drive out into the country, get alone with God and pour out my heart to Him."

In a secluded spot on a nearby lake kneeling in prayer a deep wail rose up from within, and he began to cry out, "Daddy!" It was as if he were trying to repair something that had broken long ago, trying to find his roots and identity.

Just then, the Holy Spirit brought Romans 8:15 to my husband's mind: "For you have not received a spirit of slavery leading to fear again, but you have received a spirit of adoption as sons by which we cry out, `Abba! Father!'" Father.... That word triggered pain in Don. It meant rejection. Shame. Loneliness. Abandonment. That's why addressing God as "Father" had always been awkward for him.

Much of Don's involvement in sexual perversion had been a search for the love of a father. But as the Holy Spirit spoke those words to him, my husband suddenly realized that the One he was searching for, the One who could restore him, was God, his heavenly Father. The love of God began to fill his soul, and from that moment Don began to know God in a way he never had before. For several months afterward, he would awaken at two or three in the morning, sensing God's presence so deeply that it seemed as if he could almost touch Him.

God used the counselor to open many healing truths to my husband and me. Realizing the great deficit in his childhood, Don asked God to re-parent the little boy inside him and bring him to emotional adulthood. Little by little, he severed the emotional tie to his dad that had been used to set him up to meet his needs in unhealthy ways. He was able to release his father from his bitter judgments and unrealistic expectations. (Eventually, as he worked through his grief and sadness, he was able to focus on good memories of his dad, remembering how he had labored to take care of his family. Eventually, he was even able to thank God and get in touch with a love for his father.)

We both were beginning to realize that we were responsible for our own happiness and our relationships with others. Don recognized that he no longer had to feel ashamed when he needed closeness or comfort, for God the Father was there and was teaching him healthiness in relationships with me and others.

The counselor also helped us understand why he had felt such rage against me at times and why a romantic love for me simply wasn't there. He realized that the anger wasn't about me; it was against all the hurts of his past. When I did something that reminded him of his father, he put the mask of his dad on my face and felt a bitter, intense rage which he directed at me. However, as Don experienced the love of his Heavenly Father and began releasing his pain, he found a new love that could only have been put there by God. He began to love me with the kind of selfless love a marriage deserves. We began learning to communicate our needs and feelings to one another and began working together. As we began re-anchoring our marriage, we began finding joy in our relationship. Most good memories from the first years of our marriage had been buried under bad memories from later years. Don and I had so many hurts to overcome, we had to consciously make an effort to build good memories.

Sometimes I'd find myself thinking, Maybe it would be more sensible to leave Don and start out with someone else with whom I didn't have a reservoir of bad memories to overcome. Then I would silently acknowledge that I would have to take myself—my past experiences, my weaknesses, etc.— into any relationship, and God had told me to stay put.

Something one of my friends had told me about her second marriage remained riveted in my mind, "This marriage is working better because I'm working harder on it," she had explained. "When you're Number two, you try harder." Resolving to give it my very best effort, I decided to do my part in making my first and only marriage a new marriage.

Exchanging Lies for Truth

For years, Don had participated in a lifestyle of wrong behaviors based on false ideas that he had adopted in an attempt to have his needs met and to protect himself from being hurt again. During the process of restoration, my husband couldn't always identify when he was in danger of falling back into areas of deception that could lead to danger. Realizing he needed help, Don asked me to become his partner in his restoration.

In hindsight, I personally believe that asking a third person who loved us both to be a partner in his restoration would have been much better. I don't recommend that other couples do what we did, it's harder and takes longer. However, as I learned when and how to ask my husband what his real motives were in certain situations, he better understood his patterns of addiction and see how they had worked in his life. Even then, human pride sometimes made it hard to acknowledge motives and replace long-believed, deceptive lies with God's truth.

Recognizing the enormous strides my husband was making toward wholeness, people occasionally began coming to him for counsel. I was glad to see him offering help and encouragement to others once again. However as he began counseling and discipling a certain person. I could see an emotionally dependent relationship emerging.

I voiced my concern to my husband that in the past he would develop a relationship with a person who needed him. The problem with the relationship was that the person's dependence would actually be meeting Don's own need to be close to someone who needed him.

But Don brushed aside my warning and asked me to assist him in helping and befriending that person. As I prayed about it further, I believe the Lord told me that I could not walk with my husband in that relationship.

When I shared that with Don it revealed the unhealed emotions of the addiction and he became furious. "This person needs discipling!" he exclaimed. "If you hinder the progress and this person becomes discouraged and gives up, it will be all your fault!"

"I will not try to stop you if you choose to continue counseling this person ," I said quietly. "But I cannot walk with you in it and be a part of it."

For several weeks our relationship was very strained, but one truth cemented in my spirit: Don was not God. I took very seriously the command that God had spoken so forcefully to me in the past: "Thou shalt have no other gods before Me." I resolved not to violate what I believed He was saying to me in this situation. Satan had deceived me in the past with his lie that I was not submissive if I did not obey my husband. But submission, God had taught me, was the attitude in my spirit rather than doing or not doing what my husband asked me to do.

As we prayed about the situation, the Lord began to show Don that in the past such emotionally dependent relationships had become a way for him to control and manipulate others so they would fulfill his needs for closeness. Understanding that fact was an important step in his recovery, a critical step toward living as God would have him live. After a few weeks, my husband referred that person to someone else.

I knew in my heart that God wanted His best for all of us. Therefore, it wasn't just one of us who would develop through listening to and obeying Him in the situation. God intended that it be a growing experience for each of us.

Walking In Darkness

God had promised my husband that he would be an example of

His mercy and restoration. However, for the first year after his resignation, everything seemed so dark that neither of us had much hope for the fulfillment of the promise. We stayed home a lot and didn't hear from very many believers. Except for encouragement from those few Christian leaders who committed themselves to him as he started to work through the process of restoration, it was a time of isolation for us.

Toward the end of the second year, the Christian leaders to whom my husband had submitted himself and made himself accountable believed there should be a public time of releasing him back into ministry. We had no schedule; he had nowhere to go and speak. He did short-term counseling, but he referred most people to others who were professionally trained or better equipped. We had no idea what our future would hold, but we tried to keep walking one day at a time.

As time passed, more and more invitations came to minister. People began requesting tapes. Pastors here and there began seeing the need to have someone like Don help them address the life-controlling problems with which some of them, their staff members, or members of their congregation, were struggling. God truly was carrying out His promise that Don would be an example of His mercy and restoration.

New Beginnings

It was five long years after Don's resignation before our house in Waco sold. At last, the time came when God seemed to say, "This season of your life is past. You have learned the lessons I kept you in this place to learn. Now it is time to make room for the new." We packed up our belongings, walked out the door of our house in Waco and entered the new door God was opening for us in Florida.

In Waco, where the bad seemed to outweigh the good, my husband and I had to guard against allowing our marriage to become anchored in the negative and getting stuck in the bad memories. We had learned to value the power of forgiveness in our relationship even more, realizing that it prevented bitterness from taking root.

In Florida, Don and I had so much fun together shopping, cleaning and transforming our leased condominium into a home. Happy, new memories accumulated one upon another, giving us an even stronger anchor in our relationship. We walked on the beach together. We watched giant sea turtles lay their eggs in the sand. When their young hatched out, we watched the baby turtles make their way to the ocean. Memory after wonderful memory found its own special place in our grateful hearts. My husband confided, "Now, whenever I think about our marriage, I automatically think about all the good things that are happening." That's how I felt, too.

Our move to Florida was a new beginning for us. Jamie Buckingham, the noted Christian author, became our pastor. For over two years he had been urging us to come to Florida. Out of their own failures, he and Don had a united heart to see fallen Christian leaders restored. Years before we met Jamie and Jackie, one of his books, *Soar With the Eagles*, had ministered to me in a way few books ever had. Jamie, his wife Jackie and their wonderful church made room in their hearts for us. Once again, we were part of a loving family of believers, and God gave us many dear friends. The small home group that opened their hearts and homes to us will forever remain special.

Our long journey through the wilderness lay behind us and our relationship with one another was becoming healthy and fulfilling. Don's ministry, which Satan had tried to invalidate and destroy, continued to flourish and expand.

One day while thumbing through the index cards from my "God Bag," my heart was drawn to a manna verse the Lord had given me years before. Scrawled in faded ink were these words: "You were tired out by the length of your road, yet you did not say, 'It is hopeless.' You found renewed strength, therefore you did not faint" (Isa. 57:10, NAS).

I bowed my head, too overcome to put my gratitude into words. God had strengthened and upheld me and had walked with me every step of the way. The truths He taught me on our journey had transformed my life. God's promises had outlived Satan's lies.

Chapter 11

VESSELS OF MERCY

I do not like the fiery trials of life. But of this I am certain: God knows the place to allow the test. It is His love gift to us, for it permits anything that is not of Him to be revealed. The fiery trial is sometimes the only way for us to recognize and confront the ugliness of sin still hidden within us. It is the only way to reveal the hidden flaws and weaknesses that will destroy us or disqualify us for God's highest purposes if those cracks and defects are not recognized and repaired.

God, the Almighty Potter

The first six verses of Jeremiah 18 contain some of the most precious truths in the Word of God for those of us who have been marred on the wheel of life or failed His fiery test. In those verses Jeremiah describes how, in obedience to God, he went to the potter's house, patiently awaiting a word from the Lord as he watched the craftsman at work.

The prophet was no stranger to potters and pots, for pottery making was one of the oldest crafts in Bible lands. Pottery was produced by firing clay objects to a temperature high enough to change the physical and chemical properties of the impressionable, pliable clay into a new substance with many of the characteristics of stone.

As Jeremiah sat watching, the potter threw a ball of carefully kneaded clay onto the center of a foot-powered wheel spun counter-clockwise by his hand. To Jeremiah, the clay was just a shapeless, worthless lump. But the potter looked and saw in the clay a thing of beauty, value and great usefulness. He did not simply throw the clay onto the wheel, then leave it to chance. He had both a plan and a purpose in mind. Thrusting his forearm into the spinning mass of wet, supple clay, he hollowed out the interior. Almost magically, a vessel began taking shape with only light pressure from his skillful fingers.

However, as the prophet sat in silence, thoughtfully observing the potter at work, the vessel being formed in his hands was marred. Rather than discarding the clay in which he had invested so much, the potter painstakingly reworked it into another vessel, as it seemed good to the potter to make it. "Then," writes Jeremiah, "the word of the Lord came to me saying, 'Can I not, O house of Israel, deal with you as this potter does? ...Behold, like the clay in the potter's hand, so are you in My hand...'" (Jer. 18:5,6).

Honor or Dishonor?

In Romans 9:20-23, Paul alludes to the concept of vessels of honor, vessels of mercy and vessels of wrath. When he speaks of God blinding men's hearts, making their ears heavy and "fitting" men for destruction, the apostle is attributing such works to God in a permissive sense, not in an intentional, predestinating sense, just as the potter never predestined a vessel to become a vessel of wrath. Though Paul readily affirms that God prepares men for glory (vessels of honor), he does not imply that God has ever intentionally fitted any being for destruction. An individual stubbornly rejecting God's grace and wasting his spiritual self under the influences of sin and selfishness is fitting himself for destruction by the hardening influence of his unyielding, unrepentant heart. He is like the cracked vessel which refuses to adhere to the new clay, rejecting the potter's merciful efforts to mend it.

Don't Blame God

Paul makes this point of personal responsibility crystal clear when he repeats the analogy of the Potter and the clay in a letter to Timothy:

But in a great house there are not only vessels of gold and silver but also [utensils] of wood and earthenware, and some for honorable and noble [use] and some for menial and ignoble [use.]

So whoever cleanses himself [from what is ignoble and unclean]

—who separates himself from contact with contaminating and corrupting influences—will [then himself] be a vessel set apart and useful for honorable and noble purposes, consecrated and profitable to the Master, fit and ready for any good work (2 Tim. 2:20,21, Amp., emphasis mine).

The Divine Potter has us all on His wheel, but it is you and I, not God, who are responsible for the shape our character assumes. Out of the same lump of pliable potter's clay may come vessels of honor, vessels of mercy and vessels of wrath. Some vessels may be marred, but it is not because of any mistake or mishandling by the Potter. An enemy may have slipped in some coarse, damaging ingredient, or the clay might have become contaminated through contact with the inferior and unclean. Yet if the lump of useless clay will set itself apart for the Master's use and separate itself from corrupting influences, the Potter can take it in His hands again and form a rare and lovely thing.

Rights and Differences

Our Divine Potter has the sovereign right to mold us to His will, but He has also conferred rights on the clay. We have the right to sow to the Spirit and reap everlasting life, but we also have the right to sow to the flesh and reap corruption. Like King Saul, we can harden our hearts and willfully pursue a course that fits us for destruction. Or, like David, we may choose a course that develops our souls, enables us to serve our generation and prepares us for glory.

Our hardships, experiences, temperaments and talents differ. The Potter takes all those inequalities and conditions of life into account. No merit is ascribed to a person who is what he is because of something given to him, not acquired by him. God asks only if our achievements are equal to our opportunities.

Vessels of Honor. Vessels of Mercy.

I appreciate and admire those faithful, steadfast believers who have remained unmarred through the fiery trials of life. I admire these vessels of honor who, like Joseph, Daniel , Esther and Samuel, have come through the fire unflawed—pure and holy, tried and true. Their grace under pressure inspires us all.

But I also will be eternally grateful that God values and uses vessels of mercy. Vessels like King David and Simon Peter, who cracked in the heat of temptation and trial, but humbly received the new clay necessary for their restoration and emerged strong and unscathed from subsequent firings.

The Right Response

In our Potter's nail-pierced hands, no flaw is final. No failing is fatal. The same loving Lord who convicts is also the One who can correct. He only reveals to heal.

If you and I believe those precious truths, we will not give way to hopelessness and despair when we, or other believers, fail. We will not delay the mending process we need so desperately by denying the crack's existence, attempting to conceal it, or trying in vain to fix ourselves. We will not point in horror and disgust at the flawed among us or back away from the broken vessels in our midst.

Instead of discounting and discarding the damaged, we will lend our strength and support. We will help spread the message that the flawed can be fixed. We will be approachable and trustworthy, making it easier for the weak and broken to confess their faults and come for help. We will stand by those who have fallen, encouraging them to receive the grace God gives to take responsibility for their actions, come under God's authority, become accountable and embrace the new, healing clay. As these vessels of mercy are proven and restored, we will respect their gifts, value their ministries and entrust them with places of usefulness and service in the Body of Christ.

A Promise Fulfilled

Unlike the prophet Jeremiah, I had known little about potters and pots. What I had angrily mistaken for neglectful leniency and careless indifference on God's part had actually been a demonstration of His mercy and longsuffering. While judgment and punishment knocked at the door, the Divine Potter had been patiently lingering over the impressive, but weak and unstable vessel wobbling on His wheel, stretching forth His hand and offering His mercies.

Finally, the time for firing could be delayed no longer, and the vessel was put into the kiln. As the flames rose and the temperature mounted, the worst happened. From the kiln sounded an ominous "pop" as an ugly crack appeared, and the beautiful vessel's weakness was exposed.

"I have been involved in sexual immorality.... The counselor I've been seeing...let it slip.... The board has already met. I will be meeting with them this afternoon and resigning before the church tomorrow evening. It's all over...." If I live to be 100 years old I'll never ever forget my husband's words or the traumatic series of events that followed.

But an agonizing experience that seemed so incredibly damaging in the beginning opened the way for ministry to thousands of people suffering from addictive and compulsive behaviors and other life-controlling problems. God's promise to my broken, despairing husband as he cried out to the Lord after his exposure and resignation continues to be fulfilled: Don truly is becoming an example of God's mercy and restoration.

Today, Don and I have a ministry known as Journey Toward Wholeness, conducting seminars and workshops across the nation. I am the founder and director of Homes of Hope Ministries with several residential homes for men and women.

Our ministry reaches out to hurting people struggling with all types of destructive, life-controlling problems. We can face them eye to eye, heart to heart, for though our human clay cracked in the heat of the flames, we were neither destroyed nor discarded. We can assure them that for every hurt, every flaw, God has an answer. No situation is beyond hope or help.

Broken. Filled. Mended.

I look back over all those years when my husband was wrestling with sexual perversion and I was struggling along beside him, weighted down with ever-increasing problems of my own.... Trying to build my life on sinking, shifting sand. Wanting to depend on Don for almost everything and making him my life-source. Having little or no identity. Struggling with low self-esteem and inadequate boundaries. Controlling.

Manipulating. Judging. Blaming my misery on my husband's problems. Allowing feelings to dictate how I lived. Being consumed by anger, hatred and rebellion. Stepping willfully into Satan's trap. Winding up shame-ridden and suicidal, believing I had forever forfeited God's best.

I had been tried by fire, and the flames had revealed my weak character, flawed personality and defective belief system. Now I was broken. Worthless. Angry at the fire, the ugly crack and even the Potter, I stubbornly resisted His touch, preferring to shatter into a thousand useless pieces.

But when I yielded to Him, the Master Potter prepared the flaws so they could be fixed. He carefully opened the menacing cracks and gently filled them with the healing, restoring clay of love and forgiveness, grace and truth. Then the Potter gave me the grace to embrace the new clay. As I forced my feelings, thoughts and actions to adhere and conform to it, my flaws began mending. I was forgiven. Being restored. Traces of my former failures dissolving.

I no longer fear life's wheel, His hands, my brokenness or the flaming heat, for now I know that my weak human clay must be fired or I will have no strength to stand alone, no place of service or honor.

When I was frail and flawed, one simple, powerful truth fused my broken pieces into unbroken peace: Rest, peace and joy are not determined by people or circumstances.... Rest, peace and joy come from hearing and obeying God's voice. Receiving and adhering to that truth can mend any brokenness, transform any weakness and restore any vessel.

A Vessel of Mercy

We can learn to hear and obey God. We can live our lives on the rock. Instead of becoming distracted and discouraged by people and problems, now I try to focus on His presence and promises. Choosing to walk by faith rather than being ruled by feelings. Entrusting myself and my loved ones to the care and keeping power of God. Submitting to His sovereign purposes. As I do these things, I believe the Almighty Potter will cause my pressures and responsibilities, my suffering and injustices, my circumstances and adversities to work together for good. He will use them to prepare me for His purposes and continue toward perfecting His image within me.

No weakness, no flaw, is fatal or final in God's sight. He can mend us and make us into a vessel of mercy, transforming our pieces to His peace!

* **Note From Author:** Information provided by Des Evans, Ph.D - study of the writings of Aryeh Kaplan, *The Mysteries of the Kabbalah*, under the teachings of Midat Harachamin *(Attribute of Mercy).*

For information about ordering books, please call or write about the following:

Journey Press
P.O. Box 1019
North Little Rock, AR 72115
Phone: 501-834-8908
Fax: 501-834-8910

From Pieces To Peace - By Helen Crossland

Journey Toward Wholeness - By Don Crossland
"Don's own personal story and practical insights for restoration."

Refocusing Your Passions - By Don Crossland
"Overcoming The Cycles of Shame and Addiction."